The Christian Church

James Nelson
and Juliana Gilbride

6 5 4 3 2 1

© Nelson and Gilbride
2002

Designed by Colourpoint Books,
Newtownards
Printed by W&G Baird Ltd

ISBN 1 898392 98 6

About the Authors

James Nelson has been a Head of RE and is now a lecturer in Religious Studies at Stranmillis University College, Belfast.

Juliana Gilbride (nee McNeice) is Head of RE in Rainey Endowed School, Magherafelt, and is currently seconded to the CCEA as Religious Studies Subject Officer.

The following symbols are used throughout the book to guide the reader.

Activity   **Questions**   **End of unit Questions**   Tips for exams   **Learning outcomes**

The following symbols are used throughout the book to indicate a reference to that particular denomination:

 Baptist

 Methodist

 Church of Ireland

 Presbyterian

 Roman Catholic

Photo credits:
Cover and page 108: Methodist Church, Dept of Youth and Children's Work
Camera Press: 18 (top left), 20 (left)
Concern: 10
Belfast Telegraph Newspapers Ltd: 25
Juliana Gilbride: 93
Pastor Clive Johnston: 79
James Nelson: 122
PA Photos: 20 (right), 80
Norman Johnston: 26, 28, 31, 32, 35, 36, 38, 39, 40, 41, 42, 43, 44, 45, 46, 47, 48, 49, 50, 51, 52, 53, 69, 72, 87, 121
Wesley Johnston: 23, 66
The clergy kindly provided the photographs of themselves.

Colourpoint Books
Unit D5, Ards Business Centre
Jubilee Road
NEWTOWNARDS
County Down
Northern Ireland
BT23 4YH
Tel: 028 9182 0505
Fax: 028 9182 1900
E-mail: info@colourpoint.co.uk
Web-site: www.colourpoint.co.uk

Contents

Preface and Acknowledgements

The primary intention of this book is to provide a resource for Religious Studies which directly meets the needs of the 'Christian Church' section of the Northern Ireland Core Syllabus at Key Stage 4. The Core Syllabus recommends that students study the topics in this section of the course from the perspective of at least two Christian traditions so we have incorporated the five most popularly studied traditions in order to provide variety and choice. It is hoped that the introductory material to each unit and the end of unit questions will provide students with an understanding of general issues surrounding each area of study and a framework within which to place their knowledge of specific churches.

The importance of studying the practices and beliefs of different Christian traditions cannot be overemphasised in our religiously divided society. We hope that the materials here will challenge stereotypes and provide stimulating and challenging learning experiences for the children who use them. We have tried as far as possible to represent each of the traditions included as fairly and accurately as possible and we would like to thank the clergy who kindly assisted us in that task:

Rev Graham Connor, Bloomfield Presbyterian Church, Belfast
Fr Ciaran Dallat, St Oliver Plunkett's Roman Catholic Church, Toomebridge
Pastor Clive Johnston, Magherafelt Baptist Church
Canon Stuart Lloyd, St Patrick's Church of Ireland, Ballymena
Rev Heather Morris, Dundonald Methodist Church

We would also like to acknowledge the many other individuals who kindly contributed their experience and expertise as we carried out our research for the book, some of whose names appear alongside their contribution in these pages and others who wish to remain anonymous.

A special thanks again is due to all the Colourpoint team for their sterling work.

James Nelson and Juliana Gilbride
August 2002

Reverend Graham Connor   Father Ciaran Dallat   Pastor Clive Johnston   Canon Stuart Lloyd   Reverend Heather Morris

A note regarding language

As the term 'Catholic' is claimed by several Christian denominations, the title 'Roman Catholic' is used when several churches are being discussed. However, in chapters which deal specifically with the Roman Catholic Church the term 'Catholic', which the members commonly use to refer to themselves, is used.

As all churches in this book are organised on an all-Ireland basis, the use of the word Ireland throughout is used to refer to the whole island, rather than any political entity or national state.

Introduction

A brief history of the main churches in Ireland

The origins of Christianity in Ireland can be traced back to **St Patrick** in the fifth century CE. For over one thousand years there was little change in Christian worship from one part of the island to another. It was not until the late sixteenth century, after the **Reformation**, that things gradually began to change.

The Reformation was a time of religious and political upheaval when many Europeans recognised the need to tackle corruption in the Christian Church and begin a process of change.

Some demanded such radical change that they no longer recognised the authority of the Pope and began to worship separately from the **Roman Catholic Church**. These were called **Protestants**, although, from the very beginning, there were different types of Protestants associated with different leaders who had their own ideas of how a true Christian Church should worship and what a true Christian should believe.

The result was the establishment of four main forms of Protestantism:

1. **The Lutherans**, associated with the teachings of Martin Luther.
2. **The Calvinists**, associated with the teachings of John Calvin.
3. **The Anglicans**, associated with Henry VIII.
4. **The Anabaptists**, associated with a wide variety of radicals who were more extreme than the main reformers.

The Church of Ireland

The Christians in Ireland were largely unaffected by the reforms taking place and it was not until **Henry VIII** declared himself the Supreme Head of the **Church of England** that a Protestant presence emerged in Ireland. The foundation of the Church of Ireland dates back to this period, although the Church of Ireland believes that it shares the heritage of Christianity in Ireland as far back as St Patrick, for while it took on new ideas from the European reformers it did not abandon the tradition and heritage of the Catholic Church. Therefore it regards itself as both Protestant and Catholic.

It was of course in the late seventeenth century, during the Williamite wars, that Protestants became a dominant force in Ireland. While the majority of the population of Ireland remained Roman Catholic, the members of the Church of Ireland gained a privileged position at the heart of society. In Ireland, for example, after the success of the Protestant William of Orange, you could not be a Member of Parliament unless you were a member of the Church of Ireland.

The close relationship between state and church lasted until 1869 when the Church of Ireland was disestablished, thus becoming an independent church with its own form of government. Today the Church of Ireland has over 450 parishes in Ireland in 12 dioceses.

The Roman Catholic Church in Ireland

Despite the efforts of William of Orange and others, the Catholic Church survived in Ireland. During most of the eighteenth century it was difficult for Catholics to practise their beliefs openly: priests could not wear their priestly clothes in public, Catholic churches were not allowed to have steeples or ring bells and the

Catholic people were unable to own land, receive an education or vote. It was not until **1829** that **Catholic Emancipation** was finally achieved and Catholics regained their rights and were permitted to become members of parliament. The most recent surveys of church membership show that the Catholic tradition is the largest of all the local Christian churches, with thousands of parishes which make up 33 dioceses across the island of Ireland.

The Presbyterian Church in Ireland

The Presbyterian Church in Ireland traces its roots to the **Calvinist** branch of the Reformation. Through **John Knox**, a fiery preacher noted for his plain speaking, Calvinism was introduced to Scotland. When Scottish planters came to settle in Ireland in the seventeenth century they brought their style of worship with them, and the first Presbyterian churches were soon established in east Antrim. Today the Presbyterian Church has over 550 churches in Ireland.

The Methodist Church in Ireland

The Methodist Church was originally a group of people within the Anglican Church who committed themselves to a serious, rigorous and methodical way of living the Christian life and of sharing their beliefs with others. It was because of this that they were nicknamed Methodists.

During the eighteenth century, the leaders of the Methodist movement, **John** and **Charles Wesley**, made several visits to Ireland, spreading their teaching. Methodism developed several branches after the death of John Wesley in 1791, but eventually, in **1878**, these various strands came together to form the Methodist Church in Ireland. Although numbers in the Methodist Church have declined steeply in the Republic of Ireland, there are 233 churches in Ireland, north and south, today.

The Baptist Church in Ireland

The European forerunners of the Baptist Church were a sixteenth century group of radical reformers known as **Anabaptists** (which can be translated as 're-baptisers'). They regarded the baptism they received as infants to be meaningless and were re-baptised as believing adults. They considered this to follow the example of baptism in the New Testament. They believed that individuals could be baptised only after they made a personal commitment to God and it could not be done on their behalf by parents or anyone else.

The first Baptist church in the British Isles was founded by **Thomas Helwys** at the beginning of the seventeenth century in **Spitalfields**, England. The first-known Baptist churches in Ireland were established during the seventeenth century in the Dublin area, followed by Waterford and Cork. It wasn't until much later, with the establishment of the **Baptist Irish Society** in **1814**, that the denomination really began to grow. Today in Ireland there are 109 Baptist churches, 93 of which are in Northern Ireland and 16 in the Republic of Ireland.

Activity

Using the information in this introduction, try to devise a time-line which illustrates the history of the main churches in Ireland.

Compare your time-line with other members of your class and discuss any differences that arise.

You may discover that some of the differences in your time-lines are similar to the different interpretations people have of the history of Christianity in Ireland.

The Christian year

THE CHURCH CALENDAR

Everyone loves holidays! We all look forward to special times of the year when we don't have to go to school or work and when we have time to spend with our family and friends. Traditionally our holidays in Britain and Ireland follow the Christian calendar and we associate Christian festivals such as Christmas and Easter with feelings of relaxation and celebration. However, there are other festivals celebrated by Christians and all festivals are not times for enjoyment but can also be occasions for reflection and sometimes even sadness.

The Christian year is a twelve-month cycle, but it does not begin in January like a traditional calendar; it begins with the season of **Advent** in late autumn. The table of the Church year below shows the most important festivals celebrated by Christians. Some of these are **fixed festivals**, which means that they take place on the same day every year – for example, Christmas Day is always 25 December – while others are **movable festivals**, which means their dates change from year to year – for example, Easter Sunday will always be on a different date than the year before.

The main festivals (**Advent**, **Christmas**, **Easter**, **Pentecost**) are celebrated by most Christian denominations but there are those who celebrate no festivals, some who celebrate only two, and those who celebrate these and many other special days or times such as saints' days. In general, Easter is considered to be the festival of greatest importance to most denominations.

FESTIVAL	EVENT REMEMBERED OR REASON FOR CELEBRATING
Advent	To prepare for the coming of Christ
Christmas	The birth of Christ
Epiphany	The visit of the Magi
Lent	A time of preparation for Easter
Holy Week	The last week in the life of Christ, his trials and crucifixion
Easter Sunday	The resurrection
Ascension Day	The ascension of Christ into heaven
Pentecost	The coming of the Holy Spirit, the establishment of the Christian Church
Harvest	A thanksgiving for food and crops

Activity

Using a current calendar, design a diagram of the Church calendar for this year including the months and dates of the main festivals. First consider how you will present the information, for example as a table, a pie chart or a list. Then add the information – the months, important dates, and the names of the festivals.

If you have access to the internet you could find a current calendar of the Christian year at the 'Faith In Schools' website (www.faithinschools.org). You could also design your calendar using a drawing or word-processing package and print out the results.

The meaning and purpose of festivals

The reasons why people celebrate Christian festivals include the following.

1. **To remember** – The majority of Christian festivals are based on a special moment or event in the life of Jesus. These festivals help Christians to remember the story of his life but they also draw attention to the religious importance or significance of the events. Some festivals are not associated with Jesus' life but with other events in the Bible and some help Christians to remember the lives of saints.

2. **To mark the seasons of the year** – Many Christian festivals replaced pagan festivals which marked important times of the year. For example, 25 December was associated with the pagan 'Birthday of the Sun', which marked the beginning of longer hours of daylight, while Easter was associated with the 'Festival of Spring'.

3. **To celebrate** – We all need to enjoy ourselves. Laughing, singing, dancing, sharing and relaxing are all basic human needs. Festivals are a chance to set aside time when people stop their routine activities and have some fun.

4. **To reflect and to plan** – Many Christians use festivals as a time to reflect upon their lives. For example, during Advent and Lent, Christians examine their past actions and thoughts and resolve to lead better lives in the future.

Activity

Festivals – many or few?
Look at the following list of statements about festivals and put them into two columns – arguments for observing festivals and arguments against.

- *Having a calendar keeps you organised and structured.*
- *Festivals are a distraction from true worship.*
- *There is no Christian calendar in the Bible.*
- *Marking a special event on a particular day means you are less likely to forget the occasion.*
- *Christmas and Easter are good examples of how celebrations can become more important than the religious beliefs behind the festival.*
- *It is important to remember the death and birth of Christ all year, not just at Easter or Christmas.*
- *Festivals help Christians to have a sense of tradition and history.*
- *Enjoyment and celebrations are a fundamental human need.*

Keeping these statements in mind, write an answer to this question:

Are festivals an essential part of the Christian tradition? You should consider more than one point of view in your answer.

Questions

1. *Copy and complete the list below, putting the following festivals in the correct order: Easter, Epiphany, Pentecost and Christmas:*
   (i) Advent
   (ii)
   (iii)
   (iv) Lent
   (v)
   (vi)
2. *What are the differences between fixed festivals and movable festivals?*
3. *What is considered to be the greatest festival of the Christian year? Why do you think this is the case?*

ADVENT, CHRISTMAS AND EPIPHANY

Do you remember what it was like in the weeks before Christmas when you were a young child? It seemed that Christmas Day would never come; it was a period of anticipation and excitement. These are also the feelings associated with Advent.

The word Advent literally means 'coming' and it is a time of reflection on the coming of Christ into the world at his birth. It is also a time of preparation, when Christians turn their minds to the **Second Coming** of Christ (the **Parousia**) and consider what they need to do to be ready for his return. So it is not just a time of excitement; there is also a sense of seriousness, devotion and self-examination.

Advent is four weeks long and marks the beginning of the Christian year. The first Sunday of Advent is always four Sundays before Christmas, which means it could be as early as 27 November or as late as 3 December.

In the Church of Ireland and Roman Catholic churches, purple is the colour used for vestments and altar frontals during the season of Advent. Purple is the colour of mourning and represents penance. Historically, Christians confessed their sins during Advent so that they could celebrate Christmas with a clear conscience.

Can you think of another time in the Christian year when purple might be used?

During Advent, particular readings from the Bible are used at some church services. From the Old Testament there are readings which refer to the coming of the Messiah and from the New Testament there are readings about the time leading up to the birth of Jesus.

John the Baptist is an important Biblical figure who is also remembered during Advent. According to the Bible, he was sent by God to prepare the way for Christ's first coming (Luke 3:16).

Through the scripture readings Christians focus on two important aspects of Jesus:

(1) he is the Messiah who had been foretold by the Old Testament prophets;

(2) he is the Son of God.

Activity

Look up the following passages that are read during Advent. What do they say about the coming of the Messiah or Jesus, or about the Second Coming?

Isaiah 65:17–25

Luke 1:31–35

Matthew 1:21–23

Customs associated with Advent

Many customs associated with Advent involve counting down the time until Christmas begins.

The Advent Wreath

The most familiar image associated with Advent is probably the Advent wreath. This custom involves the lighting of candles on a wreath. One candle is lit on each of the four Sundays of Advent and on Christmas Eve or Christmas Day the final candle is lit.

The circle of evergreen leaves symbolises eternal life. The flames on the candles remind Christians that Jesus is the 'light of the world'.

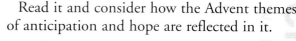

Festivals of light

Other religions also use the symbol of light during festivals. When Hindus celebrate **Divali** they put lamps and candles in their windows as a symbol of hope and to welcome the goddess of good fortune. When Jews celebrate **Hanukkah** they light a candle on each day of the festival.

Why do you think light is such an important religious symbol?

The Advent Calendar

This is a more recent tradition than the Advent wreath. The first-known Advent calendar was published in Germany in 1903. The calendar contains 24 little doors that are opened one per day from the first day of December.

Originally, inside each door was a text telling the Christmas story, but through time, pictures of angels and nativity scenes became usual. Today Advent calendars are sold in many high street shops and inside them you may find chocolate to eat!

Charity events

As Advent is traditionally a time when Christians think about how they might change for the better, many charity organisations provide opportunities for practical action. One popular event at this time of the year is the **Concern sponsored fast**.

During Advent another charity, **Christian Aid**, provides resources for churches and schools to encourage people to think about others. On the next column is a translation of an Arabic carol used in recent Christian Aid literature.

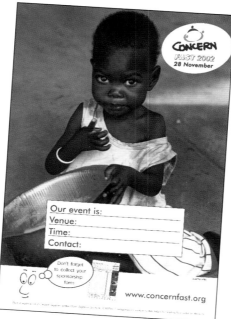

Read it and consider how the Advent themes of anticipation and hope are reflected in it.

On the eve of Christmas, hatred will vanish,
on the eve of Christmas, the earth will flourish,
on the eve of Christmas, war will be gone,
on the eve of Christmas, love will be born.

When we offer a glass of water to a thirsty person,
it is Christmas,
when we clothe a naked person with a gown of love,
it is Christmas,
when we wipe the tears from weeping eyes,
it is Christmas,
when we line a hopeless heart with love,
it is Christmas.

The meaning of Advent and Christmas

Some Christians despair that the seasons of Advent and Christmas in our society are no longer about celebrating Christ's birth but celebrating our own wealth; that shopping has replaced worshipping and supermarkets have replaced churches. This desire to 'shop 'til you drop', the feeling of never being satisfied and always buying more and more things is called **consumerism**.

Of course, we all have to buy things like food in order to survive, but consumerism describes a way of living where buying and consuming things becomes all-important.

Many Christians feel that there are dangers associated with consumerism because it leads people to believe that:

• possessions are the most important things in life;

• it is their right to buy whatever they want, when they want, without thinking about where it comes from or what will happen to it when they have finished with it;

• it's okay for God and spiritual values to take second place.

Activity

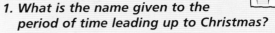

Read the article below, 'The Season of Advert', and consider the following questions:

1. What kind of society does David McMillan think we have created?
2. Why does he think the season of Advent is a good idea?
3. What do you think he means by saying that we are in danger of ignoring the "big issues"?

Questions

1. What is the name given to the period of time leading up to Christmas?
2. At Advent Christians prepare for the Second Coming of Christ. What kind of changes might they make in their lives?
3. Why is the symbol of light such an important religious symbol?
4. Read John 8:12. In what way did Jesus consider himself to be a light to the world?
5. Why do you think some charities organise sponsored fasts during Advent?

The Season of 'Advert'

We have entered the season of Advert. It used to be called the season of Advent!

Advent was a time of waiting and reflection before Christmas. It was a time of preparation before the big celebration of the coming of Jesus, God's son, born as a human being.

But now there's no waiting – just a mad drive to encourage us to spend as much as possible on stuff that's largely unnecessary and useless. What's worse, we seem so eager to oblige! Parents will get themselves into a flap and even into debt because children must have whatever they demand. Children will demand whatever the advertisers tell them they need. Ridiculous behaviour! Wherever did they learn such attitudes?

Well, actually, we taught them. Mums and dads, aunts and uncles, politicians, teachers, ministers of religion – we teach the children this behaviour.

Children imitate what they see and fairly faithfully copy how adults behave. So if it seems that the pressure to 'have' and to 'get', and to have it all 'now!' seems a bit ridiculous, we adults have no-one to blame but ourselves.

Hang on a minute though.

What kind of people are we becoming? What kind of society are we creating with this madness? We are becoming less understanding of one another, more impatient – that's why we use each other so much. We are becoming 'users', using relationships and other people as a means to satisfy our needs. We are becoming more concerned about things than people – that's why lots of elderly folks die in neglect or get 'ripped off' or mugged. We are becoming less content with the more we have.

Advent is actually a good idea. It's a good idea to have a season in which we take time out to think through some important issues. It's good to have a time when the focus shifts from me and mine to God and his. It's about time we stopped worshipping our little tin and plastic gods and ourselves and gave God his place.

When we begin to take some time to think through the Christmas story we soon discover that, even if we don't, God knows how to wait. God was prepared to work through the normal process of human development so that it took some 30 years before the man Jesus died on the cross. God is prepared to wait and give us a lifetime to come to our senses and sort out our relationship with him and then forgive us for the mess we make while taking so long to get sorted. What patience!

What a crazy bunch we are. Over the next few weeks we'll want to get drunk – tonight! We will want to have a good time – now! We will take our custom elsewhere if we don't get served – immediately! We'll be queuing up at the returns counters come 28 December to get instant refunds and meantime spend even more on instant lotteries. But we'll leave off the big issues, like giving the Creator his rightful place, until some other time. Big mistake.

When the baby whose birthday is the excuse for our crazy commercialism grew up, Luke's gospel records him saying, "Real life is not measured by how much we own . . . a person is a fool to store up earthly wealth but not have a rich relationship with God."

If his birth is worth celebrating surely his teaching's worth heeding.

Have a happy Advert – I mean, Advent!

Pastor David McMillan
Windsor Baptist Church, Belfast.

Christmas

The word 'Christmas' is an abbreviation of the two words: Christ's Mass. In the Western Church Christians celebrate the birth of Christ on 25 December, although the exact date is unknown. In the Eastern Church, Christ's birth is celebrated on the twelfth day of Christmas, 6 January.

The Christmas story

The Christmas story is very familiar to most people in this country, but there is no single version that everyone agrees on. It is told in many different ways and in a lot of cases the story that is popularly retold owes as much to tradition as it does to fact. Indeed, some of the first people to retell the story, the Gospel writers, tell the story very differently.

- Matthew says nothing of the census, the angel's visit to Mary, a manger, or the shepherds.
- Luke doesn't mention the angel's visit to Joseph or the Wise Men.
- Luke's account is written very much from Mary's point of view.
- Matthew's is written from Joseph's point of view.

Clearly, the writers wanted to emphasise certain parts that they thought were important, and when people tell the story today they continue to do the same. What most Christians agree on are the beliefs which lie behind the story:

- that Jesus was like no other child;
- he was a special gift from God;
- he would save people from their sins.

Activity

Look up Matthew 2 and Luke 2.

Make a list of the different groups of people who made a contribution to the events surrounding the birth of Christ.

What does the detail given in each gospel account tell us about the purposes of both Matthew and Luke?

Christmas traditions

Activity

In pairs, make a list of all the traditions and customs you can think of which are associated with Christmas. Can you explain the significance or meaning of the traditions? If you are unsure, the table opposite may be able to give you the answer.

There are thousands of customs and traditions that people associate with Christmas. Some are directly related to the story of Christ's birth found in the Bible. Others have been invented by Christians to help them make their celebration of the festival more meaningful or enjoyable. Still others have their origins in old pre-Christian pagan traditions. One example is Father Christmas whose origins date back to the fourth-century saint, Nicholas, who was renowned for his generosity and concern for children. However, there were also pagan celebrations even before Nicholas when a mid-winter festival took place in December.

How do Christians celebrate Christmas?

There are a variety of ways that Christians choose to mark the occasion. Many Roman Catholic and Anglican Christians attend **Midnight Mass** on Christmas Eve so that they can begin Christmas day in the proper frame of mind.

Other denominations hold a special church service on Christmas morning. This is often a **family service** and young children are encouraged to bring their toys. Christmas **hymns** and **carols** are sung and readings are carefully chosen from the Christmas story.

There are also some churches which do not have any special service. They may feel that Christmas is not an important festival or they may feel that the most important way to spend Christmas Day is with their family. Of course, a main part of the celebrations on Christmas Day, for the majority of Christians, is the giving of presents and eating a large Christmas dinner –

[go to page 14]

Custom or Tradition	Origin of tradition or reason for celebration
Santa Claus	The name comes from the Dutch for Saint Nicholas, 'Sinter Klaas'.
December 25	The date adopted by the Church for the angel Gabriel's visit to Mary is 25 March. The Church added nine months to it to get 25 December for the date of Christ's birth. This date was also used to replace the pagan mid-winter festival.
Christmas cards	Sending cards is a recent Christmas tradition that started in 1846 when Henry Cole produced 1,000 cards.
Mistletoe	In pagan times mistletoe was believed to have magical qualities. The tradition of kissing may be associated with the fact that mistletoe was a symbol of fertility.
Holly	Christians believe the holly represents Christ's crown of thorns and the berries his blood.
Christmas carols	'Carol' means ring-dance. These were songs sung at religious festivals throughout the year. They almost died out but during the nineteenth century were revived as a specifically Christmas tradition.
Christmas tree	Decorating trees took place during the pagan mid-winter festival of Saturnalia. The use of fir trees was a German custom and was made popular in this country by Prince Albert in the nineteenth century.
Nativity play	The word 'nativity' means 'birth' and in this context refers to the birth of Christ. The plays are a way for young children to remember Jesus' birth through acting out the Christmas story. Such plays are an echo of the Mystery Plays that were performed in the Middle Ages to explain the faith to those who could not read the Bible.
Crib	A model of a stable containing Mary, Joseph, the baby Jesus, the shepherds and the Wise Men. In some churches the baby Jesus is put into the crib only on Christmas Eve at a special service.

although even this is not done by everyone. Some Christians decide to give money to charity at Christmas rather than exchange gifts and some prefer to spend Christmas Day providing meals for homeless people rather than staying at home and eating too much turkey.

Activity

Read the statement below of one young person's experience of Christmas in her Presbyterian church and then discuss the following questions. You could also use the questions to design a questionnaire to find out about Christmas in other denominations.

1. Is Christmas important to you?

2. What makes it important?

3. Do you think it is still regarded as a religious holiday in our society?

4. How do you think Christians should celebrate the birth of Jesus?

Anne-Adela Walker is a teenager who attends a Presbyterian church in Belfast:

Christmas is a very important time in the life of my church. It is a time when the church gathers together and celebrates the birth of Christ. On Christmas Eve we go carol singing around the local community and give small gifts to the local residents. On Christmas morning, my church has a special service where young people bring along their new toys and show them to the rest of the congregation. We sing Christmas carols and listen to Bible readings based around the Christmas story. There is a five-minute epilogue at the end for the adults and then the service is over. It only lasts for 45 minutes and is very relaxed and informal.

Christmas is a very special time for me as a Christian. It is a time when I remember Jesus being born in a stable thousands of years ago and then 33 years later dying on the cross so that I can go to Heaven. Christmas is also a time for me to be with my family and friends. At Christmas time I get to meet up with my relatives that I don't see at any other time throughout the year. I love Christmas, especially because it's a celebration of Christ's birthday.

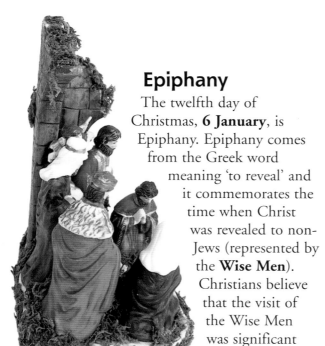

Epiphany

The twelfth day of Christmas, **6 January**, is Epiphany. Epiphany comes from the Greek word meaning 'to reveal' and it commemorates the time when Christ was revealed to non-Jews (represented by the **Wise Men**). Christians believe that the visit of the Wise Men was significant because it was a sign that Christ's birth would be important not just to Jews but for all people and nations. This concept is known as **universalism**.

The Wise Men worshipped Jesus and brought him three gifts which Christians believe have symbolic meanings.

- **Gold** was the gift for a king – Jesus is King.
- **Frankincense** was the gift for a priest – Jesus would act as a priest, opening the way between man and God.
- **Myrrh** was an oil used to anoint the dead – Jesus was going to die a significant death.

The Twelve Days of Christmas

On the first day of Christmas my true love gave to me a partridge in a pear tree . . .

You have probably heard this song *The Twelve Days of Christmas* many times, but have you ever wondered what it all means?

What have French Hens, Maids A-Milking, or Turtle Doves to do with Christmas?

The song was originally written at a time when it was forbidden to be a Roman Catholic in England and so the words in the song are a type of secret code. Each of the gifts in the song has a hidden meaning. For example, the "true love" refers to God and the "partridge in a pear tree" is Jesus.

It was too dangerous to write anything down, so the best way to help young Catholics to learn the essentials of their faith was through rhymes and songs.

The Twelve Days of Christmas is one of a number of 'catechism songs' from the sixteenth and seventeenth centuries.

Questions

1. **What does Epiphany mean?**

2. **What symbolic significance do the Wise Men have in the stories of the birth of Jesus?**

3. **Give three examples of how Christians might try to highlight the religious meaning of Christmas in their celebrations.**

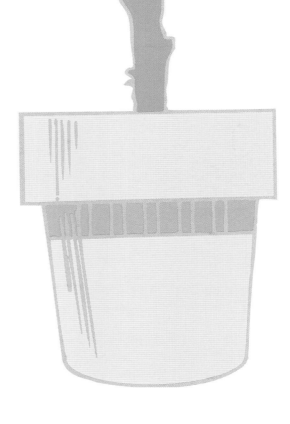

LENT AND EASTER

The importance of Easter for Christians cannot be over-emphasised. The *Catechism of the Catholic Church* says of Easter: "It is not simply one feast among others, but the 'Feast of feasts'." The festival of Easter lasts for 90 days in total. It begins with **Ash Wednesday** and ends at **Pentecost**. Lent, which begins on Ash Wednesday, lasts for 40 days (not including Sundays) and the day of Pentecost occurs 50 days after Easter Sunday.

Like Christmas, there is evidence of pre-Christian traditions associated with the Easter festival. The word Easter, in fact, comes from the name of a pagan goddess of spring, 'Eostre'.

The date of Easter

The dating of Easter was an issue that caused fierce argument among Christians in the past. Even today the Western Church (the Roman Catholic Church and all Protestant denominations) celebrate Easter on a different date from the Eastern Church (the Orthodox churches and the Oriental churches). The Western Church uses the **Gregorian** calendar while the Eastern Church uses the **Julian** calendar.

The method of dating which we currently use goes back to a decision made by the **Council of Nicea** in **325 CE**. This states that Easter Day is the Sunday following the first full moon (known as the **Paschal** full moon) after the spring equinox (21 March). Try the simple method below of working out the date of Easter.

Activity

You will need only a pencil and paper to work out the date for Easter by following these instructions.

To find the date of Easter, firstly you have to find the date of the Paschal full moon and then the date of the Sunday following the full moon. There are three main steps to follow.

Step 1: Find the Golden Number (The time of the Paschal full moon)

Choose a year from the present up to 2099. Add one to the year and divide it by 19, working out the remainder. This remainder is the Golden Number. If there is no remainder then the Golden Number is 19.

Step 2: Find the Sunday letter

Add together the following, where Y= your chosen year, ignoring any remainder in the total:

$$Y + \frac{Y}{4} + 6$$

Divide the total by 7, but this time working out a remainder.
The remainder will give you the Sunday Letter by consulting table 1.

TABLE 1

Remainder	Sunday Letter
0	A
1	G
2	F
3	E
4	D
5	C
6	B

Step 3: Find the date of Easter Sunday

Using both pieces of information from step 1 and step 2, you are now able to find the date of Easter Sunday for your chosen year using Table 2.

First look for your Golden Number in the first column. Then, look for your Sunday letter occurring in the third column after your Golden Number.

It is important to note that if your Sunday letter occurs on the same row as your Golden number you must look for the time the letter next occurs.

This is the date of Easter Sunday for your chosen year.

TABLE 2

Golden Number	Day of the Month	Sunday Letter
	21 March	C
14	22 March	D
3	23 March	E
	24 March	F
11	25 March	G
	26 March	A
19	27 March	B
8	28 March	C
	29 March	D
16	30 March	E
5	31 March	F
	1 April	G
13	2 April	A
2	3 April	B
	4 April	C
10	5 April	D
	6 April	E
18	7 April	F
7	8 April	G
	9 April	A
15	10 April	B
4	11 April	C
	12 April	D
12	13 April	E
1	14 April	F
	15 April	G
9	16 April	A
17	17 April	B
6	18 April	C
	19 April	D
	20 April	E
	21 April	F
	22 April	G
	23 April	A
	24 April	B
	25 April	C

Lent

Lent is the period of 40 days (excluding Sundays) that stretches from Ash Wednesday to Easter Sunday. It is a time of preparation for Easter, and is associated with Jesus' temptation when he **fasted** in the desert for 40 days and 40 nights; indeed it used to be a time for all Christians to fast.

This did not mean that they simply stopped eating, but certain foods like fish, eggs and milk were forbidden and people would have eaten much less food than normal, perhaps only a small meal each evening.

Today, the majority of Christians are more relaxed about observing Lent as a fast, although it is still an important part of the Christian year, as we shall see.

Shrove or Pancake Tuesday

This is the day before Lent and the two titles which it has tell us something about the significance of this day.

1. Shrove Tuesday – a day of confession.

In the Middle Ages Christians would go to church on this day to be **shriven**, meaning to receive forgiveness and absolution for the sins they confessed. The priest usually gave the person something to do to help them not to repeat the sin. This may have taken the form of a prayer.

2. Pancake Tuesday – a day of celebration.

In order to get ready for the traditional fast during Lent it was important to use up all the forbidden ingredients in the house. It was also a last chance for people to enjoy themselves before the solemn period of Lent.

In Britain and Ireland this has led to the making of pancakes, but in other parts of the world it is a day of carnivals and parties. The biggest and most famous Shrove Tuesday celebration is **Mardi Gras** in Rio de Janeiro, Brazil.

A participant in the Mardi Gras street carnival in Rio de Janeiro, Brazil.

Activity

Read Matthew 4:1–11. In what way might the temptation of Jesus be an encouragement to a Christian during Lent?

Ash Wednesday

Ash Wednesday is the first day of Lent. In the Catholic Church a special service takes place during which worshippers confess their sins and are **'signed with ashes'**. This means that the priest marks the sign of the cross on a person's forehead using ashes, which is a public way for the person to show they are truly sorry for their sins and that they intend to live a good Christian life in the future. The ashes are made from the burning of the previous year's palm crosses (see Palm Sunday on the next page). The reason for the use of ashes comes from the Middle Ages when some Christians wore sackcloth and covered their head in ashes as a form of penance.

Ash Wednesday marks the start of a period of reflection when many Christians prepare themselves for Easter. This can involve the following.

- **Prayer** – there are extra church services held during Lent in some churches when people can pray together. Others choose to spend more time in individual prayer and meditation. In both cases the main type of prayer will be confession.

- **Bible study** – different denominations may hold special Bible study groups during Lent in each other's homes. These help people to find out more about the Christian faith and how to live a good Christian life.

- **Fasting and penance** – this is both a way of showing that you are sorry for your sins and of sharing in the suffering of Christ. One way of doing penance is to give something up or to make a sacrifice of some sort. In certain cases acts of penance involve extreme hardship and pain. For example, each year in the Philippines men volunteer to be crucified like Christ for a short period of time.

However, penance can also be something more positive and more practical, such as doing extra Bible study, giving money or help to charities.

One Anglican church in America encourages its members to participate in an original activity called 'The Giving Cross'.

The Giving Cross

The Giving Cross is a tradition we at St Luke's use during certain seasons of the year (particularly Lent and Advent) to help us focus on the needs of others and, perhaps, come to a clearer understanding of our own ministries in the world.

Our parish Giving Cross is a big wooden cross that we cover with index cards, each listing a particular act of service. We put it up in the parish hall and invite parishioners to take a card or two from the cross, perform the service written on the card, and then drop the card(s) in the offering plate on Sunday. In the past, some of the services suggested have included donating blood, volunteering to work a shift at the soup kitchen, volunteering to cook and deliver a meal to a person in need, making a financial contribution to one of our outreach ministries, etc.

The Giving Cross is also easily adaptable for home use, and is a great way to focus your family (and especially children) on the ways in which God calls us to love one another. It makes a particularly good family Lenten tradition.

Mother's Day

The fourth Sunday in Lent is known as Mother's Day. Traditionally, on this day Christians thank God for how the Church has cared for them, like a mother. It is based on a statement made by St Paul in a letter to the Galatians (Galatians 4:26).

More recently Mother's Day has come to be a day when people can show appreciation for their mums and let them have a day to put up their feet and relax.

Holy Week and Easter Sunday

The last week of Lent is called Holy Week, when Christians remember particular events in the life of Christ, such as his suffering and death (often referred to as the **Passion of Christ**), and the resurrection. The most important days are **Palm Sunday**, **Maundy Thursday**, **Good Friday**, **Holy Saturday** and **Easter Sunday**.

In some denominations there are many church services held during Holy Week and in the Roman Catholic Church many worshippers carry out personal devotions, such as praying around the Stations of the Cross, to remind them of Christ's final suffering.

Palm Sunday

On Palm Sunday Christians remember the triumphal entry of Jesus into Jerusalem, when crowds welcomed him with shouts of 'Hosanna' and waved palm leaves as a sign of honour.

In some churches palm crosses are given out on this day.

Two of the traditions associated with Maundy Thursday are the distribution of Maundy money by the Queen (left) and the washing of people's feet by the Pope (below).

Maundy Thursday (Holy Thursday)

The word Maundy is not commonly used in everyday speech. It derives from the Latin word *mandatum*, which means 'commandment', and it is associated with Jesus' Last Supper with his disciples, the event Christians remember on this day. At the meal Jesus said: "And now I give you a new commandment: love one another. As I have loved you, so you must love one another" (John 13:34).

Jesus also gave a practical demonstration of his love by washing the feet of his disciples. This was an act of humility and service and Christians are encouraged to remember their duty to serve others on this day. In some churches the priest or minister washes the feet of a member of the congregation as a sign of their duty to serve the people of God. In the past the king or queen of England carried out the custom of washing poor people's feet, but now they distribute Maundy money to elderly people. Feet washing is still carried out by the Pope at a special Maundy Thursday service.

Maundy Thursday also has great importance because it commemorates the institution of the rite of the **Eucharist**. At the Last Supper Jesus instructed his disciples to eat bread and drink wine, explaining that his death would be the start of a new covenant between God and his people.

After the Last Supper Jesus took his disciples to the Garden of Gethsemane where he asked them to stay awake and pray. Jesus returned three times to find that they had fallen asleep. Shortly after this, Jesus was arrested. To remember this night, many denominations hold a prayer vigil during the night of Maundy Thursday.

Good Friday

Good Friday (also known as Great Friday), the day when Christians remember Jesus' crucifixion, is the most solemn day of the Christian year. It may seem strange that a day of such sadness is called 'good', but Christians believe that through his death Jesus achieved something great, giving all people the chance to become part of God's kingdom. Many Christians fast or abstain from meat as a sign of sorrow on Good Friday.

In the Roman Catholic Church there are several customs and traditions carried out on this day to mark its importance.

- Because Good Friday is a day of mourning normally no Mass is celebrated on this day.

- Traditionally a church service was held at 12 o'clock, aimed at helping the congregation to empathise with the pain and humiliation experienced by Christ. However, many churches have moved this service to the evening to allow more people to attend.

- Candles are extinguished and pictures are removed or covered.

- To help the worshipper to identify with the suffering of Christ, the '**Stations of the Cross**' are observed (see page 52).

In St Anne's Church of Ireland Cathedral in Belfast the 'Three Hours' from 12.00 pm until 3.00 pm is still observed. A series of 25-minute services highlight aspects of the crucifixion in music, praise, prayer, devotional readings and comments, with people coming and going as they please.

Holy Saturday

After Jesus was taken from the cross he was buried in a stone tomb. On this day Christians continue to contemplate the death of Jesus, but there is also a sense of anticipation and excitement for the day ahead, the Day of Resurrection. For this reason an **Easter Vigil** service is held on Holy Saturday night in Roman Catholic churches.

Easter Sunday

After the solemn events of Holy Week comes Easter Sunday, a day of great joy. On this day Christians celebrate the **resurrection** of Christ from the dead. Some celebrations begin at midnight on Holy Saturday while other Christians may attend a dawn service on Easter Day to watch the sun rise and thank God for Christ's resurrection. Common themes during all services at Easter are **light** and **new life**.

New Life

The most popular symbol of Easter is of course the **Easter Egg**. It symbolises Jesus' resurrection: new life breaking out of the tomb.

Light

An important symbol of Easter in the Roman Catholic Church is the **Paschal candle** which has a special role in the Easter Vigil service. This service begins on the Saturday night and at midnight the Paschal candle is lit and carried through the Church. The candle is then used to light smaller candles which are passed around the congregation.

This demonstrates that Christ, through his death and resurrection, is the light from God which has overcome the darkness of evil and that this is something which everyone can share in.

Any of the icons or statues which were covered during Good Friday are now uncovered and many churches are decorated with flowers.

The meaning of Easter

Pope John Paul II called Christians an 'Easter People' indicating the importance of this festival. Through the death and resurrection of Jesus, Christians believe people can experience God's power in their own lives; they can have their sins forgiven and receive everlasting life. This is probably the most important reason for celebrating Easter, but Jesus' death and resurrection are also meaningful to Christians for the following reasons.

1. They proved there is life after death.
2. They proved Jesus was the Messiah.
3. They fulfilled Old Testament prophecies.
4. They showed God's power over sin and death.
5. They showed how much God loved humankind.

Questions

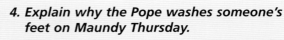

1. On what day did Jesus enter Jerusalem on a donkey?

2. Why is Lent an important time for many Christians?

3. Name four events of Jesus' life that are remembered during Holy Week.

4. Explain why the Pope washes someone's feet on Maundy Thursday.

5. How is a Paschal candle used during Easter? Explain why it is used in this way.

6. Explain the significance of Good Friday.

7. Why is Easter considered to be the central festival of the Christian year?

Activity

Sean Kelly, a teenager from Armagh, is a member of the Catholic church. Read the statements below about Sean's experience of Easter in his church.

Easter is a very important time in the Catholic Church. Holy week, in particular, is an enriching time in Armagh. On Holy Thursday people from all over the diocese come together for a Chrism Mass in Armagh Cathedral. There is a great feeling of togetherness. During this service the Archbishop washes the feet of a number of local people as a reminder of Christ's act of humility in washing the disciples' feet.

On Good Friday there is no Mass as it is a day of mourning the death of Our Lord. There are two services held – one in the afternoon at 3.00 pm where the priest remembers Christ's passion by walking around the church building and saying a prayer at each of the stations of the cross. A choir sings an anthem or response between each station as well. This is very moving and helps to remind us of all Christ went through. In the evening there is a similar service which is longer as it also includes a drama or role-play of the last events of Jesus' life carried out by the priest and members of the congregation. This gets lots of people involved and is a time of real sharing.

On Easter Saturday night there is a vigil Mass. There is normally a baptism carried out at this service. This is one of the only times where a baptism takes place during a public service, so it is very special. I particularly enjoy this service because of the symbolism associated with it. Everyone is given an unlit candle as they enter the church. The service begins in darkness and then the Archbishop comes carrying a lit Paschal candle. As he walks through the church members of the congregation light their candles from the paschal candle until the whole building is ablaze with light.

Easter Sunday is focused towards the joyful celebration of Christ's resurrection through the Mass. It is very uplifting and joyful and an appropriate conclusion to the whole period of Easter.

I enjoy the celebration of Easter much more than that of Christmas because it is less commercialised. Easter, to me, is the focal point of the religious year because it reminds me of the suffering of Our Lord. Jesus made the ultimate sacrifice for us by dying on the cross and I think it is helpful to have special services to remind people of that.

Now either discuss the following questions in groups, or use them to design a questionnaire for your friends and family and then share your findings with the rest of the class.

1. Is Easter an important time in your church?

2. What makes it important?

3. Do you think it is still regarded as a religious holiday in our society?

4. How do you think Christians should remember the death of Jesus?

Activity

Read the newspaper article 'Religious holiday to be axed' and discuss the questions that follow.

Religious holiday to be axed

Schools are to be told to scrap Easter holidays and replace them with a non-religious 'spring break' as part of a fundamental overhaul of the way children are taught.

Despite objections from the Church of England and Christian pressure groups, supporters of the proposals say a specific Easter holiday is incompatible with a modern school system because it is on a different date each year. Moving to a fixed holiday would reduce teacher stress and pupil truancy and improve exam results.

The proposals say schools should be more ready to celebrate non-Christian festivals such as Divali and the end of Ramadan. Head teachers will be allowed 10 'flexible days' each year to hold holidays which reflect the ethnic make-up of the school.

Kamal Ahmed, political editor
Observer, Sunday 27 May 2001

1. In groups, discuss the idea of replacing Easter with a spring break which is at the same time every year. Do you think it would make Easter less important if it were no longer a school holiday?

2. One Christian, Martyn Eden of the Evangelical Alliance, said in response to the idea: "We will strongly oppose any move to bring in the changes."

What reasons do you think he would give to support his opinion?

ASCENSION AND PENTECOST

Ascension Day

Ascension Day is 40 days after Easter Sunday and marks the occasion when Christians believe Jesus returned to heaven – you can read about it in Acts 1:1–11. The writer of Acts also tells us that before he left, Jesus promised the disciples that they would soon receive the gift of the Holy Spirit.

Ascension Day is always on a Thursday and is not a public holiday. Because of this, it is not widely celebrated or particularly well known outside the Christian Church. In the Roman Catholic Church and the Church of Ireland, Christians mark the day by celebrating the Eucharist.

Pentecost

At Pentecost Christians celebrate the coming of the Holy Spirit, which was promised by Jesus. Pentecost is also said to be the birthday of the Christian Church because through the power of the Holy Spirit the disciples began to spread the message of Christ's death and resurrection, and many thousands of people were converted.

Pentecost means 'fifty' and it falls 50 days after Easter.

The symbols of Pentecost displayed in banner form.

Another name for this festival is **Whitsun**, an abbreviated form of 'White Sunday'. In the early Church it was a time for baptisms and so it became known as **Whit Sunday** because of the white robes worn by the newly baptised.

Pentecost provides an opportunity for Christians to reflect on the gifts of the Holy Spirit. When Pentecost is celebrated in churches, the symbols representing the Holy Spirit are often talked or sung about and displayed.

Look at the symbols of the Holy Spirit displayed in the banner on page 23. What do you think they say about the Christian understanding of the Holy Spirit?

Questions

Read Acts 2: 1–13 and in groups discuss the following questions.

1. **How do you think the disciples might have been feeling after the ascension of Jesus?**

2. **What way do the disciples change when the Spirit arrives?**

3. **Christians do not agree on what exactly happened on the day of Pentecost, but we know that, in the Old Testament, wind and fire are symbols of God's presence. What do you think the writer of Acts is trying to tell us about what happened on this day?**

Questions

1. **What does the Ascension commemorate?**

2. **Give two names for the Christian festival that celebrates the coming of the Holy Spirit.**

3. **How many days are there between Easter and the coming of the Holy Spirit?**

4. **Why is Pentecost an important event in the Church calendar?**

5. **"If Pentecost was made into a public holiday people would want to learn more about its significance."**

   Do you agree or disagree with this statement? Give reasons for your answer.

HARVEST FESTIVAL

Harvest refers to the time, during autumn, when farmers traditionally brought in the crops that supplied their community with food for the rest of the year. Although fresh food is now supplied to supermarkets and shops from around the world throughout the year, Christians believe it is still important to remember that God created the world and to thank him for all his gifts of nature. Many churches take the opportunity to do this at a **Harvest Thanksgiving service**, the date of which is decided by individual churches.

The purpose of this service is not only to thank God for the abundance that is enjoyed by many in the affluent world, but also to raise awareness of the hunger that exists in other parts of the world, encouraging Christians to give to those in need.

Origin of the Harvest Festival

Harvest festivals are common in many cultures around the world. The origins of the festival celebrated by churches in Ireland are probably found in two different sources.

1. A pagan celebration of Mother Earth feeding her people was traditionally celebrated in the autumn. It was not until 1862 that an equivalent celebration of harvest became official within the Church. The pagan celebration was held in August and was known as **Lammas Day**. (Perhaps you've heard of the **Ould Lammas Fair**, which is held in Ballycastle, County Antrim, each year.) In Church history, Lammas Day became the day when the minister blessed the bread made from the first ripe corn and then celebrated communion.

2. The Jewish festival of **Sukkot** (also called the **Feast of the Tabernacles**) is a harvest festival, still celebrated by Jews today. It is a time of thanksgiving to God for the beauty of nature and the food that has been provided. It recalls a tradition when the Jewish people would set up tents in their fields to live in while they gathered in their crops, so they wouldn't waste time going to and from home during this busy time of the year.

The Ould Lammas Fair!

On the last Tuesday of August each year the famous Ould Lammas Fair takes place in Ballycastle, Co Antrim. It dates back to the seventeenth century and attracts thousands of visitors. If you go you'll find dozens of stalls selling toys and souvenirs as well as the traditional foods dulse and yellowman.

Activity

Read the following references and write a few sentences explaining why many Christians remember the Harvest Festival each year.

- *Genesis 1:29–30*
- *Leviticus 23: 39–43*
- *Psalms 107:33–8; 104:10–18*
- *Matthew 6:25–34*

Questions

1. **'We plough the fields' is a famous hymn by M Claudius often used at Harvest services. Look at the verse below taken from this hymn and suggest what you think Christians might thank God for at a Harvest service.**

   All good gifts around us,
   Are sent from heaven above,
   Then thank the Lord, O thank the Lord,
   For all his love.

2. **The Harvest service from Dundonald Methodist included the baptism of an infant. Why might this have been a particularly appropriate service for a baptism?**

3. **Look up the Bible reference which was read at the service. Can you suggest how the minister in her sermon could have made this relevant for a Harvest service?**

The meaning of Harvest

Increasingly, Christians in Great Britain and Ireland feel that giving thanks at a Harvest Festival for an abundance of food and water makes them more aware of people in other countries who have much less. During the service the minister may pray for those countries where starvation is a reality and a collection might be taken for one of the charities involved with the developing world.

What happens at a Harvest Thanksgiving service?

At a Harvest Thanksgiving service the congregation usually brings gifts of food and flowers to decorate the church building as a sign of their thanks to God. These gifts may later be taken to the elderly or to members of the congregation who may not be able to attend church due to illness.

Here is an example of a Harvest service, held in Dundonald Methodist Church

- Introit
- Call to worship
- Hymn 'We plough the fields'
- Prayer
- Baptism
- Hymn 'See Israel's gentle shepherd'
- Children's story and song
- Offering and dedication (children leave for Children's Church)
- Bible reading, John 7:37–44
- Prayers for others
- Hymn 'For the fruits'
- Sermon
- Hymn 'O Lord of Heaven'
- Benediction

Some congregations even go so far as to bring items into church at Harvest which can be sent directly to people in need after the service. The **Container Ministry** is a good example.

Container Ministry

Container Ministry is a branch of the Methodist Missionary Society, Ireland. Its warehouse receives new or nearly-new goods to send to countries in the developing world. It is staffed by volunteers and items such as books, computers, tools, clothing, hospital equipment are donated by Church members.

Sometimes at Harvest time congregations run shoebox or aquabox appeals when a young person might fill a shoebox with a toy, pencils, paper, rubbers, a ruler and a torch or an adult might fill an aquabox with clothing, toiletries and kitchen utensils. William Carson helps to coordinate the Container Ministry work:

> Container Ministry is a war on waste in this country that becomes a war on want in other less privileged countries. It converts our words of thanks into words of charity. It brings world hunger, homelessness and need closer to us to be part of our thankful response for the surplus food we have.

Questions

1. **Give two reasons why Christians celebrate Harvest.**

2. **"The Harvest festival deserves a greater place in the Church Calendar because it is a practical festival." Do you agree or disagree with this statement? Give reasons for your answer.**

3. **Some people think the name 'Harvest festival' is out of date and no longer appropriate. Can you suggest a suitable alternative?**

FEAST DAYS AND SAINTS' DAYS

As well as the major festivals throughout the Christian year there are also many other special days, or **feast days**. These days are usually associated with either a saint, Mary the mother of Jesus or a less well-known event in the life of Jesus.

These are celebrated in the Roman Catholic Church and Church of Ireland more than other denominations, but even these churches do not agree on celebrating the same number of special days.

> ### Feast days and Saints' days celebrated in the Catholic Church include:
>
> **Fixed days**
> The Annunciation (26 March)
> The Transfiguration of the Lord (6 August)
> Assumption (Feast of Mary) (15 August)
> The Birth of Virgin Mary (8 September)
> All Saints' Day (1 November)
>
> **Movable days**
> Corpus Christi
> Sacred Heart of Jesus
> Immaculate Heart of Mary
> The Feast of the Immaculate Conception

What is a saint?

The word 'saint' is used in the Bible to mean Christians in general. For example, in the letter to the Philippians Paul writes, "To the saints" – but through time it came to be a title reserved for a special few. These were individuals who had led a very holy life or had shown great devotion to God in the way they lived.

Many of the first saints were **martyrs** – people who gave their life for their beliefs, eg St Stephen – but others were remembered for their achievements in spreading the gospel or showing Christ-like love and humility in the way they acted.

There are two main reasons why saints' days are kept and why they are regarded by many Christians as important.

1. **To help people remember** – celebrating saints' days and feast days are a way of ensuring that special people or important events are not forgotten.

2. **To give Christians good examples** – saints are the heroes or role models of the Church and when the stories of their lives are retold they can be an inspiration to those who hear them.

In addition to these main characteristics of a saint, the Roman Catholic Church believes that:

- saints are **intercessors**, which means that they can assist the Christian in prayer. Because saints are in heaven they "can contemplate God, praise him and constantly care for those whom they have left on earth". Therefore Catholics believe that "we can and should ask them to intercede for us and the whole world" (*Catechism of the Catholic Church*, 2683);

- **relics** (clothes, bones and objects) associated with saints are of special importance. This possibly arose from the desire of early Christians to preserve the bodies of martyrs from being burned and discarded by the authorities in an undignified way.

How does one become a saint?

An official list of saints is called a **canon of saints**. The Church of Ireland and other Anglican churches decided at the Reformation in the sixteenth century to close their canon of saints. This means that it is no longer possible for anyone to become a saint within these denominations, although they still remember and celebrate those already canonised (made saints) such as St Paul, St Patrick and St Andrew.

The Roman Catholic Church has continued to add to the list of saints, but they have very strict rules about who can become a saint. First of all, the person must be dead! This is so that the whole life of the person can be considered.

Secondly, there must be clear evidence of the individual's specialness, such as miracles performed by the person or associated with their name. The process of weighing up all the evidence is very lengthy and involves many experts and independent witnesses.

There is also a person at every meeting nicknamed the **devil's advocate** whose job it is to query and doubt all the evidence presented. Only if the person can overcome all these obstacles can they eventually become a saint.

Activity

Examine the statements below and make notes on why it is important for some Christians to remember saints and why other Christians don't remember saints.
In pairs or groups discuss your own opinion on the following statements.

We do not normally celebrate saints' days, although significant church festivals are marked, such as Christmas, Easter and Harvest. Saint Patrick's Day is encouraged to be a time of prayer for peace.
Heather Morris, Methodist Church

We celebrate some saints' days to remind people of the broad sea of faith to which they belong, to remind them of those who have gone before who are faithful, and in some way to remind them that all Christians are saints, because everyone is called out to serve God in some form.
Stuart Lloyd, Church of Ireland

We don't celebrate saints' days because we think all Christians are saints and it is wrong to consider some better than others.
Graham Connor, Presbyterian Church

Saints' days are special because the lives of saints provide examples of how to live the Christian life and they also show that there are many different ways of living a Christian life.
Father Ciaran Dallat, Catholic Church

St Theresa of Lisieux (1873–1997)

Theresa was born into a devout Christian family and at the early age of 15 became a nun at the Carmelite convent of Lisieux.

During her short life she experienced much personal sadness, including the death of both of her parents, but she had a strong faith and was devoted to the religious life. One of the most important moments in her spiritual life was a vision of Christ that she experienced as a child.

At the age of 23, Theresa began to write an autobiography of her spiritual experiences called *The History of A Soul.* Within the year she died of tuberculosis. Theresa did not regard herself as a spiritual giant, yet her writings became extremely popular due to her honest and straightforward way of speaking about spiritual things. In a letter she admitted to not being able to understand very intellectual religious writing but says "it is enough to realise one's nothingness, and give oneself wholly, like a child, into the arms of the good God".

Because of her child-like faith she has become known as the '**Little Flower**' and continues to have a special place in the hearts of many who identify with her simple but deep and sincere spirituality. St Theresa's feast day is 1 October.

St Patrick

St Patrick is well known as the patron saint of Ireland who brought Christianity to the island in the fifth century. But how much of what we know about him is true and how much is myth?

It is safe to say that there are more questions about Patrick than there are answers. However, it is now generally agreed that Christianity had arrived in Ireland before St Patrick, maybe through a man called **Palladius**. It is also agreed that many of the stories associated with Patrick, such as the driving out of the snakes, are myths. The reason Patrick is so well known and liked is probably because of two of his writings which have survived until today – *The Confession* and *The Letter to Coroticus.*

St Patrick as depicted in a 1961 postage stamp from the Republic of Ireland.

When we read these writings we get a clear idea of the kind of person Patrick was – humble, warm, kind yet hardworking and devoted to his mission to convert the Irish to Christianity. Patrick admits that he is a "poor sinner" but he tries his best and battles on even when his job is difficult and he feels like giving up.

Through his writing, Christians see that Patrick is in many ways like an ordinary person, yet because he is obedient to God he can achieve great things. It is this example that Christians find so inspiring.

The celebration of St Patrick's Day has become a great social event in both parts of Ireland and in many cities in the USA. St Patrick's Day is 17 March.

Questions

1. **Why is it important for the Church to remember the lives of famous Christians?**

2. **"Every Christian should be remembered as being a saint when they die." Do you agree or disagree with this statement? Give reasons for your answer.**

3. **"St Patrick's Day is just an excuse for people to spend a day in the pub!" What do you think? What might be a suitable celebration of St Patrick?**

END OF UNIT REVIEW

End of unit questions

1. How do you think Christians benefit from the celebration of festivals?

2. "The modern Christian Church dwells too much on past religious events." Discuss this statement using examples from at least two major and one minor Christian festivals.

Activity

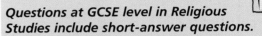

Worshippers from different religions use symbols to express ideas, beliefs and feelings during the celebration of festivals. One of the most important and common symbols is light. Use this exercise as a class to try to discover the power of this symbol.

a) Clear all books and pens away from your desks and arrange yourselves into a circle or several circles, depending on numbers, around a table with a candle.

b) Try to relax by closing your eyes and stilling yourself; meanwhile your teacher will light the candle.

c) Open your eyes and look at the burning candle for a few moments. What thoughts and feelings come to mind? What does the flame represent?

d) Staying in your circle, write your ideas down and then share your comments with others in the group.

e) Can you suggest why lighting candles is an important part of many religious ceremonies?

f) As a follow-up to this activity you could find out about the stories associated with the Jewish festival Hannukah (the miracle of the oil-lamp) and the Hindu festival Divali (the story of Rama and Sita). What does light represent in each story?

Learning outcomes

As a result of studying this unit you should:

– understand the importance of festivals;

– reflect on the significance of the main Christian festivals;

– examine key concepts associated with each festival (for example, forgiveness, thankfulness, penitence and joy);

– reflect on the significance of saints for Christians today.

Tips for exam success

Questions at GCSE level in Religious Studies include short-answer questions.

When completing a short-answer question it is important to be brief and accurate in your response.

It is also important, however, to check to see if you are being asked for more than one piece of information or if you are required to give a reason to justify your response.

In an exam you can get a clear idea of how much information you are required to give by looking at the marks available for the question.

Church buildings and furnishings

INTRODUCTION

There are many churches of different shapes and sizes to be seen throughout Northern Ireland. As part of your studies you may have the opportunity to visit some church buildings which will provide you with an insight into the lives of the people who worship there. One thing that will probably strike you if you go on a church trail is the number of differences that can be found from one church building to the next.

By observing such differences in architecture, layout and style we can learn something about what is important to those inside.

Church architecture

Activity

Try to describe the appearance and design of some churches near you. You could organise a quick class survey to ask questions such as:

Does the church have a special shape?

Does it have a tower or spires?

Where is the church situated?

Does it remind you of any other type of building? What is the entrance like?

How old do you think the building is?

It is important to share your results. Discuss how the churches in your area are similar or different. Can you give any reasons to explain why they are similar or different?

It is not possible for us to study all the types of architecture in church buildings, but there are some which are more common than others and we will consider five of these in particular:

cruciform, **barn-style**, **hall and tower**, **circular**, and **cathedrals**.

Cruciform

Cruciform means **cross-shaped**. This design highlights the importance of Jesus' death on the cross. Each part of a cruciform church also has a special name:

- the **chancel**, which usually contains the altar, sanctuary and choir;
- the **transepts**, or cross aisles, which are often used for side chapels;
- the **nave**, which is the main part of the church where the congregation sits.

Barn-style

A barn-style church is **rectangular** in shape, allowing the eye to be drawn to the front of the church where the pulpit takes centre stage. This style is used by denominations who focus on the importance of preaching the word of God. It has also been adapted in some cases to include a balcony to increase seating capacity.

Hall and tower

This is similar to a barn-style church with the addition of a **tower**. A tower suggests strength and reflects the Christian belief expressed in the Bible, "God is our shelter and strength, always ready to help in times of trouble" (Psalm 46:1). A hall and tower design could be considered to symbolise that the church is a place of refuge.

Circular

Some more modern designs are built in the shape of a **circle** or **oval**, stressing the equal importance of all the people who worship there. Sharing together in fellowship is a vital part of the worship of such denominations.

Cathedrals

This type of building is unique to the Roman Catholic and Anglican Churches and is the most important building in a diocese (the geographical area under the supervision of a bishop – see chapter 6). In Northern Ireland the city of **Armagh** is famous for its cathedrals, both of which are dedicated to St Patrick. The Church of Ireland Cathedral, which is medieval in design, is a nineteenth-century restoration built on a thirteenth-century shell.

The Roman Catholic Cathedral in Armagh was originally designed to be a cruciform building with a large square tower in the centre. However, during the famine of 1846–7 work was stopped and when it began again in 1854, a new architect changed the design to a Gothic style, introducing the tall twin spires which can be seen throughout the city.

The Roman Catholic Cathedral in Armagh shows how the design of a building can be strongly influenced by when it was built and the type of architecture popular at the time, such as classical or Gothic. Usually these different styles are used for a purpose. For example, a classical style suggests grandeur and design, while a Gothic style conveys mystery and holiness.

Both cathedrals of Armagh are dedicated to St Patrick: pictured left is the Roman Catholic cathedral and below is the Church of Ireland cathedral.

Activity

Copy and complete the following grid. An example has been done for you.

Shape/Features	Symbolism
Cruciform	
Circular	
Plain and simple building	*Conveys the message that God does not require a great building for worship. He identifies with the weak and sinful.*
Tower	
Cathedral	
Modern	
Gothic	
Barn-shaped	

The interiors of St Patrick's Church of Ireland, Ballymena (right) and Magherafelt Baptist Church (below).

Worship the Lord in the Beauty of Holiness

Church furniture

One of the ways we can learn about the beliefs of a denomination is through the type and location of church furniture found inside a building. Furniture can vary from being **plain** and simple to grand and **ornate**, but in every case it adds to the atmosphere of worship that is important to a particular denomination.

The location of furniture is a way of portraying what is central to their beliefs. For example, the pulpit in a Presbyterian church is the largest and most visible piece of furniture, which indicates that the reading of the Bible and the preaching of a sermon are central aspects of worship.

Images and icons

One very obvious difference in the decoration of Christian churches is between those who use images of Christ in their worship and those who don't. An artistic representation of Christ, the Virgin Mary or a saint which is used in worship is called an **icon**. Among the churches in Ireland there are three main positions on this issue.

a) Those that display images of Jesus, the Virgin Mary, the disciples, saints and perhaps certain Biblical scenes around the church on stained-glass windows, in pictures, on cloth banners and as statues. This is typical of most Roman Catholic churches. The images act as visual aids for the worshippers and direct their thoughts to God.

Father Ciaran Dallat from St Oliver Plunkett's Church in Toomebridge explains:

The images in our church evoke a story about God which we already know, and they invite us to respond to the story of what God has done.

b) Those that display images of Jesus, the disciples and Biblical scenes in stained glass, but not usually in picture or statue form. This is typical of Presbyterian and Methodist churches. The Church of Ireland is similar, although they also include images or carvings of saints, but not of Jesus. In general, these churches have come to view the use of art in churches positively. The Reverend Graham Connor of Bloomfield Presbyterian Church explains:

Traditionally, the use of pictures, cloth banners or stained glass would not in the past have been encouraged in the Presbyterian church; it would have been seen as a distraction. However, we now want to use them to encourage people to worship.

c) Those that have no pictures or images of Jesus, the disciples, saints or any Biblical scene in the church. This is typical of Baptist churches which believe that any image in a church would be a distraction from worship and could also be dangerous by becoming the focus for worship, instead of God. Pastor Clive Johnston comments:

We have no images in our churches because images of God are forbidden in the second commandment in Exodus 20:4. Any image is the product of someone's creative imagination and so, no matter how beautiful, is not a true representation. We worship when the Holy Spirit brings the truth of God to our minds, which moves our hearts, and lights our soul to adoration.

Flags

Flags are a common feature in Church of Ireland and Presbyterian churches in Northern Ireland, although Christians within these denominations are divided over whether flying or displaying flags in churches, particularly militaristic or national flags, is a good idea.

Displaying the Union Jack, for example, is regarded by many as a symbol of remembrance for those who died in the two world wars.

Others, however, feel that to display the Union Jack brings politics into the church and has the potential to divide or offend people.

Activity

Use the statements below to have a group or class discussion about icons, pictures and flags in churches. One person (perhaps the teacher) should read each statement out while the members of the class or group decide whether they strongly agree, agree, disagree or strongly disagree with the statement.

The discussion begins when each person explains the reasons for their opinion on each statement.

1. *Icons and pictures in a church distract the worshippers from true worship.*

2. *Images of Christ on a cross help worshippers to focus on Christ's suffering and remember the importance of his death.*

3. *Displaying military flags in a church shows proper Christian respect for those who sacrificed their lives for our freedom.*

4. *If some churches want to fly the Union Jack they should keep it on the inside of their buildings so no-one can be offended by it.*

Activity

Look at the pictures of the interior of two churches shown opposite (you may also want to think of church buildings you have visited in the past).

In small groups try to make a list of different types of furniture which you might find in a church. Can you suggest why these pieces of furniture are present in a church?

Church buildings – grand or simple?

Christians have different opinions on the religious significance of church buildings. For some, the building itself is very important because it is a place which has been set apart as the **House of God** and should be treated with great reverence and respect. Also, as a sign of devotion to God, the building should be built with materials of good quality and furnished to a high standard.

Other Christians believe that God is present in all places and that his presence in church should not be regarded as special or different from his presence in someone's house. Therefore it is not important for the building or furnishings to be of expensive materials.

But most Christians are likely to agree that:

- the church is primarily the people rather than a building. In New Testament times there were no churches like those today, so when the word 'church' is used by Bible writers it always refers to people. Paul, for example, saw the church as a '**body**' (1 Corinthians 12:12–26) which has Christ as its head. The main part of the body is made up of individual people who, like the parts of the human body, each have a different purpose but which work together to enable the body to function well.

- a church building is important because worship would be more difficult without it. The first Christians met for worship in one another's houses. If a house was big enough, a room was often set aside as a special place for worship. It would contain a table and the Christians continued the tradition started by Jesus of meeting to share a meal.

With the expansion of Christianity, whole houses were set aside as meeting places, and eventually it was possible to have purpose-built buildings designed to suit the needs of the congregation and to enhance the experience of worship.

Activity

Look at the following comments made by different clergy in Northern Ireland concerning the importance they place on their church building. In groups note:

- two contrasting opinions and reasons for such views;
- which opinion you most agree with and why.

Baptists see the people of God as being the church. It would be common for them to refer to their church as a 'meeting house' rather than a church. The building is important because it provides an appropriate place to hear the Word of God and share fellowship with God's people. However, where Baptists worship is not as important as how they worship. Jesus said that those who worship God must worship in "Spirit and in truth".

Pastor Clive Johnston, Baptist

The stones of the building contain the faith of the people over the years. People will talk about an atmosphere within the building or it being a 'Holy Place'. There is something of that in the building which you might not be able to catch if you didn't have a building. In a sense it can be regarded as a 'sacred place'.

Canon S Lloyd, Church of Ireland

The church building is a place where the people of God can gather. In the Old Testament in particular we can see that the presence of God was associated with particular places. The church building has significance in the lives of many people in the congregation, because here they perhaps came to faith or were married. The building thus has many faith memories attached to it . . . However, all that being said, the church is not simply a building; it is the people of God and that would be our emphasis. There is no limit to where God may choose to meet people and make Himself known to them.

Reverend Heather Morris, Methodist

The building has great significance in the lives of the congregation who were baptised or married here and may have buried loved ones from here. We certainly cherish our building and couldn't do our work in the way that we do if we had no buildings. However, it is only a building. It is a building where the people of God meet, a building which we cherish and want to care for, but we don't see it as being more sacred than any other building.

Reverend Graham Connor, Presbyterian

Our church building is a sacred building. As it is God's house we try to create a special atmosphere of respect through the building and furnishings. However, you only have to cross the water to England to find the local Catholic church might be used as a multi-purpose hall by the local primary school through the week or as a disco on a Saturday night for the young people. Church buildings can be multi-functional, although, in my opinion, it is also important to keep some reserved space at the altar and the tabernacle.

Father Ciaran Dallat

Now use your notes to write a response to the following question. In your answer you must show that you have considered more than one point of view.

"Church buildings should not just be used for worship."

In your answer you might consider some of the following uses:

- *sporting activities;*
- *social functions (concerts, bingo, discos, youth clubs);*
- *community groups;*
- *schools.*

Magherafelt Baptist Church

BAPTIST CHURCH

Many Baptist church buildings are unusual in that they may not look 'church-like' from the outside. Generally, Baptist church buildings are **plain**, both inside and out, and they could be described as **functional** – that is, they are designed to meet the practical needs of the congregation. Some Baptist churches have fixed pews while others use chairs that can be stacked together at one side so that the building can

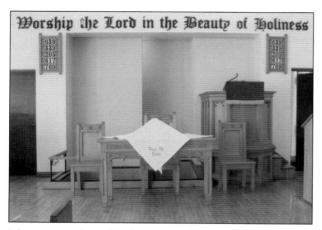

The communion table (centre) and pulpit (right) in Magherafelt Baptist.

double-up as a sports hall or meeting place. Churches with fixed pews tend to have a separate church hall or additional rooms where church groups such as 'mothers and toddlers' or youth clubs can run activities.

In this chapter and in others which focus on the Baptist Church we will be looking at the example of one church – **Magherafelt Baptist** – to help you understand what a Baptist church is like. It is important to remember that no two Baptist churches are exactly alike and, while they share some common features, each one is unique.

The Baptist Church in Magherafelt is close to the town centre. From the outside it is a plain rectangular building, with a small car park, surrounded by trees. There is also a separate church hall, but this is some distance away and is used for a youth club and for meetings for the elderly. It has a refurbished kitchen, a small games room and a lounge.

The entrance hall is quite large, leading into toilets (including one for the disabled), three Sunday School rooms, a crèche and a small room that is used for practical administration, such as photocopying.

Main features

Pulpit

One of the most prominent features in the Baptist Church is the pulpit. It is usually to be found on a platform in the centre at the front. However, in Magherafelt Baptist the pulpit is located to the right of the Baptistery (see photograph). The prominence of the pulpit shows the importance Baptists place on the Word of God. They believe that preaching is one of the main ways that God speaks to his people.

The Baptist Church also has a reading desk, called a **lectern**, which is to the left or right of the pulpit. It is often used instead of the pulpit because it brings the pastor closer to the people.

Communion table

The communion table in the Baptist Church is close to the congregation, which emphasises the importance of meeting and sharing. The table is made of plain wood, suggesting that simple worship is acceptable to God, and there is often an appropriate Bible verse inscribed along the front.

It is in front of the pulpit because Baptists believe that everything flows from the Word of God, even communion.

Baptistery

Baptists believe that baptism is an outward expression of an inward change. It is a sign that a person has become a Christian and so great emphasis is placed on the baptistery in a Baptist church.

Baptists believe that **immersion** is the only acceptable method of baptism; therefore they use a large tank instead of a font. In Magherafelt Baptist the baptistery is placed to the left of the pulpit and is an open tank (see photograph opposite). However, in other churches it may be covered and only be visible and filled with water during a service of baptism. There are usually steps at the side of the baptistery to allow easy access into and out of the water.

Other features

Scripture text

Above the pulpit in Magherafelt Baptist church there is a scripture text which reads, "Worship the Lord in the Beauty of Holiness" (Chronicles 16:29). This is to help the congregation in their preparation for worship and to act as a reminder of the importance of worship. While it is common for Baptist churches to have a scripture text displayed, the text varies from church to church.

Music

Music is an important part of worship. Most Baptist churches have an organ and a piano.

In Magherafelt Baptist the organ is on the left at the front of the church while the piano is on the right.

There is also a worship group who play guitars, keyboard, violin and a flute to accompany the singing during some services.

Audio-visual displays

While most Baptist churches have access to overhead projector facilities, others, including Magherafelt Baptist, also use PowerPoint presentations for both sermon points and as a means to display the words of hymns and choruses.

Flowers

Flowers are often found displayed in front of the organ or piano in the Baptist church. In Magherafelt Baptist Church there is a rota for the arrangement and display of flowers.

Hymn boards

There are wooden hymn boards on the walls at the front of the church in Magherafelt, one on each side. These tell the congregation what hymns and choruses will be sung during the service.

Collection plates

Some Baptist churches use a wooden collection plate to collect an offering from the congregation on a Sunday morning.

In Magherafelt Baptist a bag is used instead of a plate so that others can't see how much you are giving.

Other Baptist churches don't take an offering during the service but prefer to have boxes at the back of the church where people can put an offering as they leave.

Questions

1. *How would you describe the style of a Baptist church building?*

2. *What importance do Baptists place on the Word of God? How is this reflected in the position of the pulpit and lectern?*

3. *Explain what the design and position of the Communion table in the Baptist Church says about their beliefs.*

4. *Why do Baptists use a baptistery instead of a font for baptising? How does the baptistery differ from one Baptist church to another?*

5. *Explain how worship is enhanced in a Baptist church through features other than the communion table, baptistery or pulpit.*

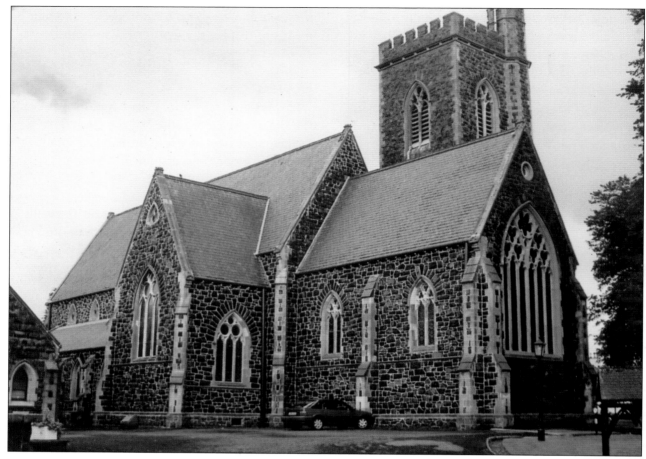

St Patrick's Church of Ireland, Ballymena.

CHURCH OF IRELAND

Church of Ireland buildings can vary greatly in style – from cathedrals to Portakabins! The Church of Ireland churches in Ballymena, Co Antrim, are a good example. There are three churches in the parish of Kilconriola and Ballyclug – St Patrick's, Ballymena; St Patrick's, Ballyclug; and St Columba's, Dunclug. (It is very common for a Church of Ireland church to be named after a saint.)

St Patrick's, Ballymena, and St Patrick's, Ballyclug, are typical of traditional Church of Ireland churches. They are stone buildings set in large grounds and are built in a traditional style – St Patrick's, Ballymena, is a cruciform shape and St Patrick's, Ballyclug, is a hall and tower design. St Columba's, by contrast, is a

prefabricated building which is used as a multipurpose hall for worship, clubs and societies. It is situated on the edge of a large housing estate and has only enough space for a small car park at the side of the building.

In this chapter, and in others which focus on the Church of Ireland, we will be looking at the example of one particular church – **St Patrick's, Ballymena** – to help you understand what a Church of Ireland church is like. It is important to remember that no two Church of Ireland churches are exactly alike and while they share some common features, each one is unique.

St Patrick's, Ballymena, is near the town centre and incorporates a large main building for worship as well as two church halls. The main church building includes a **vestry** (where the minister goes to dress and prepare for a service), a **choir room** and a **bell tower**. The church halls have a range of facilities, including a stage and a kitchen which are used by a variety of clubs and societies associated with the church. The halls also house the parish office.

The cruciform shape of St Patrick's reflects the Church of Ireland's attempt to hold in balance the importance of 'word' and 'sacrament' in their worship, and this is also seen in the position of the furnishings.

- The font is positioned at the back of the church, near the west door.
- The holy table is positioned at the front of the church, facing east. This represents an east–west axis.
- The lectern is positioned at the front of the church, at the north side.
- The pulpit is positioned at the front of the church, at the south side. This represents a north–south axis.

Joining these two axes together creates the shape of a cross. The cross holds together the word and sacrament.

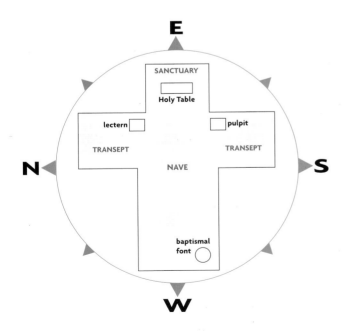

Main feature

The communion table in St Patrick's Church of Ireland, Ballymena.

Holy/Communion table

The holy table is usually a large, elaborately carved wooden table. It has a prominent position in the Church of Ireland and stands in the sanctuary of the church. In St Patrick's the sanctuary is raised above floor level, highlighting the importance of the holy table and giving the message that it is an honour to approach the table. Communion rails surround the holy table where the congregation can kneel when they come forward to receive Holy Communion.

The holy table may be covered by special cloths, the colour of which changes throughout the Christian Year. Such colours represent key events in the Christian calendar.

The sanctuary in St Patrick's, where the holy

Liturgical Colours
White – Christmas
Green – Trinity
Purple – Lent/Advent
Red – Pentecost/Saints' Days

table is situated, faces east to symbolise the rising of the sun which is representative of Jesus' resurrection. Jerusalem, the place where Jesus died, is also found in the east, so the position of the holy table has double significance. The holy table is some distance away from the congregation, reinforcing the holiness of the sacrament of communion. However, in some churches the holy table has been moved closer to the congregation to encourage more active participation within worship.

The lectern in St Patrick's Church of Ireland, Ballymena (above) and that in St Mark's, Newtownards (below).

Font

In St Patrick's the font (pictured above) is positioned beside the west door (entrance) and is the place where baptisms are carried out. This part of the church is referred to as the **baptistery**.

The position of the font in the Church of Ireland is important because it symbolises a person's entry into the family of God through baptism. The font is made of marble or wood and may have symbols engraved on it, for example, a dove symbolising the Holy Spirit.

Pulpit

The pulpit in St Patrick's is positioned on the right-hand side as you face the holy table. Its purpose is for preaching sermons and it is raised so that the congregation can see the minister.

In the Church of Ireland pulpits are made of wood or stone and may have elaborate carvings of Christian symbols to add to their beauty.

In some churches there is a **pulpit fall** hanging from the pulpit, the colour of which will once again coincide with the season in the church's calendar.

Lectern

The lectern is used for Bible readings. In St Patrick's the lectern is an ornate reading desk made from stone, although in the Church of Ireland it is commonly made in the shape of an **eagle**, like the one pictured opposite. The eagle is perched on a globe and its wings are outstretched to hold an open Bible. This is highly symbolic: the eagle is a majestic bird showing the importance of the Word of God; the outstretched wings represent the gospel being carried throughout the world, which is represented by the globe upon which the eagle is perched. The eagle is also symbolic of St John, the fourth evangelist.

Other features

Bells

Bells are a traditional feature of many Anglican churches in Ireland. They are situated in a tower or spire and their purpose is to call people to worship. In the past, people did not have watches and so relied on the bells to remind them it was time for church.

St Patrick's Church in Ballymena is proud of its long tradition of **bell-ringing**, a skill which has been passed down through many generations.

Prayer Desk

Services in the Church of Ireland are conducted from the prayer desk. In St Patrick's the prayer desk is situated at the front of the sanctuary of the church, near the pulpit.

The clergy use different service books for different occasions, such as the *Book of Common Prayer*, and these are kept on the prayer desk.

Organ

Music is an important part of Church of Ireland worship. The singing of hymns, psalms and canticles is led by the organist and choir.

The organ is often placed at the front of the building, as it is in St Patrick's, Ballymena, where it is to the left of the communion table.

A banner showing Bridget, Patrick and Columba.

Flags and banners

It is common to see flags displayed inside a Church of Ireland. These may be flags of organisations associated with the Church, such as the Mothers' Union, or in Northern Ireland the Union Jack, which is regarded as a symbol of remembrance for those who died in the two world wars. The Union Jack (in Northern Ireland) and other flags, such as the St Patrick's Cross, are sometimes flown from flagpoles outside Church of Ireland churches to mark special occasions. There are strong feelings within the church about whether this is a right or wrong thing for a church to do, and so the decision is left to each individual parish.

In St Patrick's Church in Ballymena there are flags of several army regiments and church organisations displayed, as well as the banners of three saints: Patrick, Bridget and Columba.

Questions

1. **Describe the symbolism of the buildings and furnishings in a cross-shaped Church of Ireland.**

2. **Explain how the style and location of the communion table highlights the sacrament of communion in the Church of Ireland.**

3. **Give two examples where liturgical colours are used in the Church of Ireland.**

4. **Explain the symbolism for Anglicans of:**

   (a) the font;

   (b) the lectern.

5. **Explain why flags might be on display in a Church of Ireland.**

Dundonald Methodist Church.

 # METHODIST CHURCH

Many Methodist churches in Ireland date back to the nineteenth century and reflect the traditional style of that time. Others, such as Dundonald Methodist Church, are modern in design, allowing them to be more multi-functional.

In this chapter and in others which focus on the Methodist Church we will be looking at the example of one particular church – **Dundonald Methodist** – to help you understand what a Methodist church is like. Remember that no two Methodist churches are exactly alike and while they share some common features, each one is unique.

Dundonald Methodist Church occupies a prominent position on a hill in the middle of Ballybeen estate. It was built in the late 1960s and comprises a large entrance hall which has doors leading to the other parts of the building, including the main sanctuary for worship, a kitchen, an office and a church hall.

On entering, one of the first things you notice are the wooden ceiling struts, which are meant to lift your eyes upwards, symbolising the lifting of one's eyes towards God.

The original design of the church was simple and stark. However, over the years some carpets have been laid and some items added to enhance worship, for example a lectern and a cross.

Main features
Pulpit

The pulpit is one of the key pieces of furniture, reflected in its raised position at the front. This shows the importance placed on preaching and Bible teaching in Methodism, which was encouraged by the example of **John Wesley**.

For the same reasons, the lectern is also given a prominent position at the front. It is from here that members of the congregation read, lead in prayer or speak. This shows the importance of the participation of everyone in worship services.

[go to page 44]

The reading desk (left) and pulpit (right, behind the drums) in Dundonald Methodist Church.

Dundonald Methodist Church's communion table.

Communion table

The communion table (pg 43) is usually a simple, wooden table which has words such as 'This do in remembrance of me' carved on the front of it.

During communion, it is covered with a cloth and holds the elements of bread and wine. The cloth is plain white, although it may be embroidered with Christian symbols. In front of the communion table there is a rail where people come forward to receive communion.

A communion service is held at least once a month in the Methodist Church and is an important part of their worship.

Dundonald Methodist is designed in a way which does not make the communion table seem less important than the pulpit. The pews are slanted in order that both the pulpit and the communion table have equal prominence.

Font

Methodists believe in **infant baptism** so baptisms are carried out at a font which can be made from stone or wood and is usually positioned at the front of the church. Some people like this location because it is a reminder of the importance of children in the life of the church. In older Methodist churches, the font is situated to the side of the church.

Other features

The entrance area to Dundonald Methodist church.

Entrance

The entrance is a significant part of many Methodist church buildings.

In Dundonald Methodist Church, members gather in a large entrance area to talk before and after the services on a Sunday.

Coffee is served about once a month to encourage the congregation to stay and chat. This is a reflection of the importance of fellowship within the church. People have the chance to get to know one another, both spiritually and socially and this is particularly important for new members or guests.

Music

Within Methodism music is very important. In the past the **hymns** of John and Charles Wesley were an important way in which new Christians learnt about their faith. Many of the Wesleys' hymns are contained in the Methodist hymnbook.

Some of the older Methodist churches have large pipe organs to accompany the hymns.

In addition, many Methodist churches have a **worship band** which includes a variety of different musical instruments to accompany the singing.

A plain wooden cross is the centrepiece in Dundonald Methodist.

Audio-visual displays

In many Methodist churches you will find a screen at the front of the church which is used for the projection of the words of various hymns and choruses. This screen is also used for announcements and sermon points.

Banners

Banners proclaiming different spiritual truths are displayed in Methodist churches. These reflect important aspects of the life of the church and therefore have a symbolic significance.

Cross

Many Methodist churches have a plain cross on display at the front of the church which reflects the importance of Jesus' resurrection.

Questions

1. **How might the style of building and position of the furniture in Dundonald Methodist Church help to enhance worship?**

2. **How does Dundonald Methodist Church make use of the entrance to their building? Explain why it is a significant part of the church for those who worship there.**

3. **Describe a typical communion table in a Methodist church.**

4. **How does the type of furniture used for baptism inform us of the beliefs Methodists hold concerning baptism?**

5. **Why is music an important part of the Methodist tradition?**

Bloomfield Presbyterian Church.

PRESBYTERIAN CHURCH

In the seventeenth century Scottish settlers brought their faith – Presbyterianism – to Ireland. The churches they built were generally in keeping with the style of the Scottish Presbyterian churches. These were traditionally **plain** in design and referred to as **meeting houses** which reflects the Presbyterian belief that the building is simply the place where the people meet to worship.

Many Presbyterian churches in Ireland were originally designed in the barn style – a plain, rectangular building with little decoration. However, through time these churches have been altered and adapted to suit changing needs.

In the past, for example, choirs and organs were popular and this affected the use of space and the seating arrangements. As populations increased there was often a need for larger church buildings. To cope with increasing numbers some churches were built to include a horseshoe-type **gallery**.

Bloomfield Presbyterian Church in Belfast is a good example of a large, barn-style church with a gallery as well as a choir and organ area.

In this chapter and in others which focus on the Presbyterian Church we will be looking at Bloomfield Presbyterian to help you understand what a Presbyterian church is like. It is important to remember that not all Presbyterian churches are exactly alike and Bloomfield has some unique features. For example the pews on the ground floor are slightly curved and there is a rail around the front of the choir area.

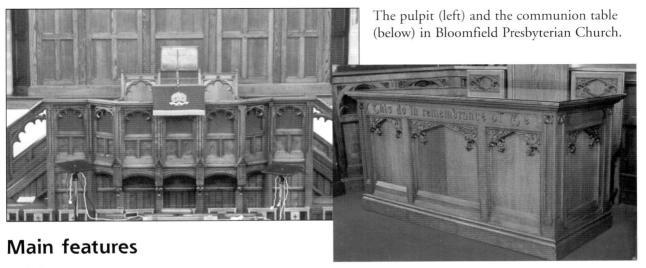

The pulpit (left) and the communion table (below) in Bloomfield Presbyterian Church.

Main features

Pulpit

The pulpit is the single most important piece of furniture in the Presbyterian Church. This is where the minister preaches the Word of God. It is a large wooden structure which is positioned at the front and middle and is slightly raised (pictured above). The reason for this is because Presbyterians meet to worship under the authority of the Word of God.

In some Presbyterian churches, services commence with the elders carrying in the Bible and placing it on the pulpit. This is very symbolic and shows that the Word of God is central to their worship.

Hanging from the pulpit is a piece of material called the **pulpit fall**. A picture of the **burning bush**, the symbol of Presbyterianism, is embroidered on the pulpit fall, along with the words *Ardens Sed Virens*. This phrase means 'Burning but not consumed' and represents the church shining for Jesus Christ but never burning out.

Communion table

In Bloomfield Presbyterian Church the communion table is positioned at the front of the church in the centre and is close to the congregation. This emphasises communion as a 'sacrament of fellowship'. The purpose of the communion table is to hold the communion elements of the bread and wine. It is placed below the raised pulpit because God's word is of utmost importance to Presbyterians, who believe that the sacrament of communion comes from the Word of God.

In Bloomfield Presbyterian the communion table is made of wood and the phrase 'This do in remembrance of me' is carved along the front. These words are taken from 1 Corinthians 11:24 where Paul gives instructions concerning the Lord's Supper. These words form part of the liturgy of a Presbyterian communion service. There is a large chair along with a number of smaller chairs assembled behind the communion table and during a communion service these are occupied by the minister and elders.

Font

In Bloomfield Presbyterian the baptismal font is positioned at the front of the church to the right-hand side. It is made from wood and holds a small silver-coloured bowl which is used to carry the water for the baptism of infants.

Lectern

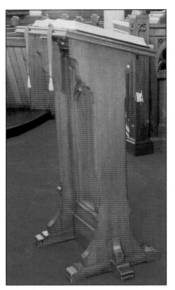

This is a small reading desk which is level with the congregation. It is at the front on the opposite side to the font.

In Bloomfield Presbyterian the lectern is used in the morning service by a member of the congregation to give a reading and by the minister to give the children's address.

In the evening the minister often conducts the entire service from the lectern as there are not as many people there.

Other features

Aisles

There is no central aisle in most Presbyterian churches. From the beginning, clerical processions did not form part of Presbyterian worship, even during their communion services, so today two aisles usually divide the seating.

Stained-glass windows

Some Presbyterian churches have one or two stained-glass windows, eg a picture of an eagle or a symbol of the Holy Spirit. Such windows may have been presented as a gift from a member of the congregation or tell something of the history of that church.

Flags

In Bloomfield Presbyterian there are two Union Jack flags on display, which are the 'colours' of the two uniformed organisations associated with the church, the Boys Brigade and the Guides.

Not all Presbyterians are happy with flags being present in a church, particularly because

Presbyterians believe that their church should remain totally independent of the state.

Banners

Bloomfield Presbyterian employs a variety of visual displays and banners at different times of the year. These are used to remind the congregation of a Christian festival or a simple spiritual truth, eg 'Jesus is Risen'.

Traditionally, such displays would not have been encouraged in the Presbyterian Church, being seen as a distraction. However, today more people are beginning to regard them as an aid to encourage people to worship.

In Bloomfield, computer-aided visual displays, such as PowerPoint, are also used every Sunday.

Questions

1. **Read Exodus 3 and 2 Timothy 2:16–17. How do these verses explain the Biblical basis for the importance Presbyterians place on the pulpit and the word of God?**

2. **(a) What is a 'pulpit fall'?**

   (b) Describe the significance of the burning bush displayed on Presbyterian pulpits.

3. **Choose two pieces of furniture found inside a Presbyterian church building and explain their significance.**

4. **Why do some Presbyterian churches have flags on display in their church building?**

Saint Oliver Plunkett's Roman Catholic Church, Toomebridge.

✝ ROMAN CATHOLIC CHURCH

The design of Catholic churches underwent great changes during the twentieth century. Traditionally, they were built in the shape of a cross and were decorated in a very ornate way. However, in recent times Catholic Church buildings have come to be circular or oval in shape and tend to have a simplicity in their style.

Many of these changes were a direct result of an important ecumenical (worldwide) Catholic conference called the **Second Vatican Council** (1962–66, known as **Vatican II**), which recommended many changes in an attempt to update the practices of the church and restate its beliefs in a way that would make them relevant to modern times.

The Catholic churches in the parish of

Duneane in Co Antrim and Co Londonderry are good examples of the different styles of architecture in the Catholic Church. The parish includes three churches: the Church of the Sacred Heart, Cargin; the Church of Our Lady of Lourdes, Moneyglass; and the Church of Saint Oliver Plunkett, Toome. Cargin is **cruciform** in shape with the altar at its centre, whereas Moneyglass is a traditional cruciform with the altar at one end. The Toome church, which is near the centre of the village in pleasant grounds, is rectangular outside but inside the people are gathered round the altar.

In this chapter and in others which focus on the Catholic Church we will look in particular at the **Church of Saint Oliver Plunkett** in Toomebridge to help you understand what a Catholic church is like. While Catholic churches share many common characteristics, it is important to remember that each one is unique in its own way.

The altar is the central, and dominant, feature in St Oliver Plunkett's Roman Catholic Church, Toomebridge. The ambo (reading desk) is to the left and the presidential chair to the right.

Main features

Holy water font

When you enter the porch of St Oliver Plunkett's church one of the first things you see is the holy water font. This is found in all Catholic churches and can either be built into the wall or may be on a stand. The congregation dip their fingers into the water and make the sign of the cross when they enter and leave the building. This reminds them of their baptism and reaffirms their faith.

In this part of the church you will also see notice boards giving details of forthcoming services and events or details about overseas mission and pilgrimages.

Altar

When you enter the main body of the church in Toome the most noticeable feature is the altar. This is the name given to the communion table and is where the priest celebrates the **Eucharist**

(communion). It is probably the most prominent feature in every Catholic church.

In the past, before the Second Vatican Council, the priest celebrated parts of the Mass with his back to the congregation. Since then in most churches the altar has been moved forward to be closer to the congregation, with the priest facing them throughout the service.

The altar in Toomebridge is at the exact centre of the church making it very accessible to the people. It is particularly helpful in allowing children to see what is happening. The position of this altar also provides a sense of togetherness, with the priest standing among the people, rather than above them.

The altar is symbolic as it is a reminder of Christ's sacrifice on the cross. As a piece of furniture it is reminiscent of the sacrificial altar which was a key feature of the Temple at Jerusalem at the time of Jesus. Catholics believe that the celebration of the Eucharist is not just a memorial of Jesus' Last Supper but also a re-enactment of the last events in Jesus' life.

The altar may be made be of wood or marble. In Toome, it is made of black marble.

Tabernacle

The Tabernacle is a special box which is located behind the altar. After Mass the **consecrated bread** (sometimes called the **Blessed Sacrament**) is placed inside the Tabernacle. Catholics believe that Christ is really present in the bread and therefore it cannot be thrown away but is stored in the Tabernacle. Preserving some bread also has a practical use as the consecrated bread may be taken to those unable to attend, perhaps because of illness.

But, more importantly, preserving consecrated bread in a Tabernacle also means that Christ is always present in a special way within the church. The Tabernacle is therefore a focus for those entering the church during the day, perhaps to pray or reflect upon their lives.

Catholics will **genuflect** (bend their knee) in the direction of the Tabernacle because they believe Christ is present through the mystery of the Eucharist. A red light, the sanctuary lamp, shines as an indication to show those entering the church that the consecrated bread is inside the Tabernacle.

Presidential chair

During the Mass the priest will sit in this chair when he is not leading the service from behind the altar.

Ambo

This is the name given to the reading desk or lectern in the Catholic Church. From here the Bible is read at each service.

Baptismal font

The font is where baptisms are carried out. The Catholic Church carries out **infant baptism**, although adults can also be baptised. The font is generally a fixed piece of furniture and in older Catholic churches it is found near the door, at the back of the church, to symbolise baptism as the entrance into the Christian Church. However, today, because many Catholic churches are circular in shape, the font is found nearer to the front, at one side, and close to the congregation.

Other features

Paschal candle

The Paschal candle is also known as the Easter candle in the Catholic Church. It is a very large candle which is decorated with important Christian symbols, such as the letters Alpha and Omega, the first and last letters of the Greek alphabet, which symbolise the belief that God is eternal.

During the Easter vigil, the candle is lit and carried up through the church, reminding the people of the light of Christ's resurrection overcoming the darkness of the tomb. Therefore the Paschal candle is a symbol of Christ rising from the dead.

The Paschal candle is also lit during baptisms. An ordinary candle is lit from the Paschal candle and given to a godparent on behalf of the child. This is a symbol of the light of faith being given to a child at baptism.

Stations of the Cross

The stations of the cross are unique to the Catholic tradition. Each of the **14 stations** represents a stage in the last events of Jesus' life and his journey to the cross. They may be carved in wood or stone or simply painted as pictures.

The Stations of the Cross are not normally used in the celebrations of Mass throughout the year. However, during Lent and Holy Week many Catholics visit their local church to meditate on the Stations of the Cross and use them as a focus for prayer.

They will stop at each station and reflect upon what Jesus went through on their behalf. In some churches there is a fifteenth station which depicts Jesus' resurrection.

Two of the stations of the Cross: The women of Jerusalem mourn for Jesus and he comforts them; Jesus falls a third time.

Icons and statues

Crucifix

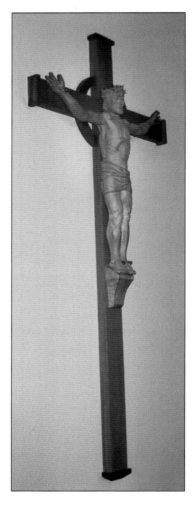

A crucifix is an artistic representation of Christ on the cross. It symbolises the suffering of Jesus and reminds Catholics of the significance of Christ's death.

A statue of the Virgin and Child in St Oliver Plunkett's, Toomebridge.

Candles

The lighting of candles is an important part of the Catholic tradition and is a symbolic way of showing devotion or respect.

Catholics often light candles in memory of a relative who has died or to honour a saint. For this reason statues of saints are often situated near the candles. Normally, the candles are kept in a rack and are found near the altar.

In Toomebridge the candle stands are located on both sides of the altar along the back wall.

Confessionals

Traditionally the confession box was a cupboard-like structure where the priest sat behind a screen to hear confessions from the people.

In more modern churches this has been replaced by an open-plan room (a 'room of reconciliation'), which is a small room off to the side where the priest hears a confession face to face.

In Toome there is a small room where people choose either to talk 'face to face' or from behind a screen.

Mary

Mary, the mother of Jesus, is given an important place in the Catholic Church. She is not worshipped but rather **revered** because she is regarded as being the 'Mother of God'.

Statues or icons of Mary show her wearing a red garment, which symbolises her humanity. Over this is placed a blue cloak, which symbolises the divinity God placed upon her when he gave her the task of giving birth to his son.

Prayers are often recited in honour of Mary, such as the **Hail Mary**.

Questions

1. *Explain the function of the two fonts in a Catholic church.*

2. *Describe how the position of the altar (communion table) has changed in Catholic churches since the Second Vatican Council. What impact do you think this has made on the atmosphere of worship in these churches?*

3. *Why is the altar the most prominent feature in a Catholic church?*

4. *Explain how icons, pictures or candles might help a person to worship in a Catholic church.*

END OF UNIT REVIEW

End of unit questions

1. Why do Christians consider church buildings to be important?

2. Church buildings have differing architectural styles. Explain, using examples from at least two denominations, the reasons for this.

3. Using at least two examples, explain how the location of church furnishings can vary in different denominations. Explain the reasons for the differences.

4. With reference to examples, explain how church buildings can contribute to the life of the community.

5. What are icons? Explain why some Christians might find them valuable in worship.

Activity

The changing church

Churches will continue to change and adapt, both inside and outside, to suit the needs of their congregation and to incorporate new forms of worship. Clergy often look for ways to make changes which will improve or add to the atmosphere of worship.

Imagine that you are an architect and have been commissioned by a local church to design a new building for worship. Your task is as follows:

1. Collect information about the kind of church the congregation would like. If time permits, this could involve interviewing several members of a particular congregation who represent different groups within the church. Otherwise you can use the general information in this unit to make your decisions about the type of building a particular denomination might like.

2. Design a church plan which includes the location of the main pieces of furniture within the church.

3. Write a report which explains what you have done and, most importantly, why, stating clearly how the design would meet the needs of the congregation.

Learning outcomes

As a result of studying of this unit
– you should know about styles of architecture in church buildings;
– you should understand the reasons for differences in architectural style and interior design of churches;
– you should form an opinion about key issues relating to church buildings and furnishings.

Tips for exam success

'Church buildings and furnishings' tends to be a very popular choice for coursework at GCSE. Here are some important points to remember when planning to write any piece of RE coursework.

1. Plan a clear structure, using headings and sub-headings, which relates directly to the question.

2. Decide where you can get resources or information for your topic. There is a good chance your teacher will be able to guide you. For any piece of coursework on 'The Christian Church' it is a good idea to visit the churches you will be writing about. If possible, this could include a visit when a service is being held.

3. Make notes from your resources. You might also use information gathered through questionnaires.

4. Begin writing according to your plan. If you are quoting from this book or other textbooks, use speech marks.

5. Check your spelling, punctuation and grammar. (This is referred to as 'quality of written communication' by examiners.)

6. Submit your first draft.

7. Listen carefully to the advice of your teacher and make appropriate changes to your work.

8. Complete your piece by adding any pictures or photographs and designing a cover sheet.

9. Acknowledge your sources in a bibliography.

10. Keep to your deadlines!

Worship

3

INTRODUCTION

When Christians worship they show **adoration**, **admiration** and **affection** to God through what they think, say and do. There are a huge variety of ways in which they express themselves, for example by praying, singing, moving and reading together.

Activity

Using the experiences of class members or interviews with church members, try to find examples of the different types of prayers, songs, movement and books used in different churches.

No two churches are the same when it comes to worship and every Christian has their own ideas about the best or most appropriate ways to worship. In fact, many splits and arguments have occurred throughout the history of the church over what is the best way to worship.

It would be impossible to list all the types of worship used in Christian churches in Ireland, so we will look at four main styles. It is important to remember that these are not the only ways of worship and some churches may be happy using one or more of the types below.

1. Formal or Liturgical worship

Roman Catholic and Church of Ireland churches are most likely to use this style of worship. Services follow a clear pattern and use **pre-written prayers** and **creeds** contained in special books. Roman Catholics use the *Missal* and the Church of Ireland use the *Book of*

Common Prayer, or the more modern *Alternative Prayer Book*. The collective term for prayers, creeds and instructions contained in a book for worship is the **liturgy**.

Those who worship in this way regard the liturgy as very special as it is based on the Bible and was written by holy, godly people who thought very carefully before writing the words. Speaking to God, they believe, is not something done lightly and when done in public should follow a proper and respectful form.

Another reason for using a liturgical style of worship is that it forms part of the **tradition** of the church. The tradition of the church is to be treasured because it has been passed down as a result of much thought and prayer. It has stood the test of time and, many argue, if it was not something which pleased God, he would not have allowed it to continue.

Christians who prefer this style of worship argue that just because worship has a clear structure does not mean it has to be boring. In fact, liturgical worship always requires the congregation to participate through saying prayers or reciting creeds as well as standing, sitting, kneeling and walking to the altar rail to receive the Eucharist.

They also believe that during a service there is still room for individual expression and variety. In support of this style of worship they often point to the Bible where there are traces of liturgical or set forms of words used during worship. For example the Israelites were commanded to recite certain words when making offerings (Deuteronomy 26: 3–15) and Jesus told his disciples that they should use his form of prayer as an example (Matthew 6:9–13; Luke 11:2–4).

2. Structured worship

In other churches worship is less book-based, but there is a general routine followed from week to week which is led by the minister or pastor. This is the case in many Presbyterian and Baptist churches. Worshippers in these churches believe that they have flexibility in their worship and are able to express themselves better in their own words. Much of the prayer is **extemporaneous**, which means it has not been written down in advance.

There may be times in these churches when they use creeds or set forms of prayer, such as the **Lord's Prayer**, but this is usually only in one small part of the service. Christians who prefer this style of worship believe that it is orderly and respectful, providing opportunities for individual expression and variety.

3. Leaderless worship

When some Christians, such as the **Brethren** or **Quakers**, meet to worship they do not have a minister, pastor or vicar who leads the service. During their main Sunday service, anyone who wishes to contribute can do so (although in the Brethren tradition women must not speak during worship). Someone might say a prayer, choose a hymn, read from the Bible or give a short sermon. Also, silence plays an important part in this style of worship, particularly for the Quakers.

For those who prefer this type of worship, the idea of the '**priesthood of all believers**' is very important. This is based on passages from the Bible such as 1 Peter 2:9 ("You are the chosen race, the King's priests") and Galatians 3:28–9 ("You are all one in union with Christ Jesus"). They believe that each individual Christian can speak directly to God and the structure of worship should be decided by the Holy Spirit rather than by a priest or minister.

They believe that this style of worship is like the worship of the first Christians, as in Acts 2, and that it follows the example Christ gave during his last supper when he shared bread and wine with his disciples, saying "Do this in memory of me."

4. Pentecostal/Charismatic worship

In general, this style of worship is very **lively**, and can range from enthusiastic singing, clapping and the use of modern musical instruments to dancing, flag-waving and moments of strong emotion. Christians who attend Pentecostal churches (such as the Elim Church, Assemblies of God or Church of the Nazarene) or Charismatic churches (such as the Christian Fellowship Church or King's Fellowship) are most likely to worship in this way. Christians who prefer this type of worship believe that worshipping God should be joyful and uplifting – not lifeless, formal and dull. They believe they are following examples of worship described in the Bible, such as Psalm 149 which says, "Praise the lord! Sing a new song to the Lord . . . Praise his name with dancing; play drums and harps in praise of him".

The word '**charismatic**' comes from a Greek word, *charis*, meaning gift. Worship which is charismatic is often associated with three special gifts of the Holy Spirit used during worship:

- **the gift of prophecy** (giving guidance for the future);
- **the gift of tongues** (speaking in an unknown or heavenly language);
- **the gift of healing** (receiving divine help for physical, mental and emotional ills).

Each of these is described in the Bible as taking place during worship in the earliest Christian churches and some Christians today believe they should still be an important part of worship.

Activity

Music and worship

Try to find examples of music used in worship.

You could look for tapes, CDs, videos or websites and make a presentation to the rest of the class to show how different types of music are used in worship.

Try to explain why each piece might be meaningful for the worshippers involved.

The use of the Bible in worship

All of the Christian churches featured in this book believe that their worship is Bible-based, yet the way in which they use the Bible during worship is very different.

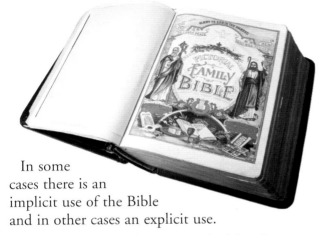

In some cases there is an implicit use of the Bible and in other cases an explicit use.

Explicit use – Bibles are supplied for the congregation or brought to church by the worshippers and each person will follow the Bible readings in their own text and occasionally refer to it during the sermon.

Implicit use – The use of the Bible by the congregation may not be obvious to an outsider but extracts from the Bible are read from the pulpit, and the liturgy used throughout the service contains many references and extracts from the Bible.

Another difference regarding the Bible and worship concerns the use of a **lectionary**. This is a book which states what passages of scripture should be read each week during public worship.

A lectionary has a cycle of either two or three years, so that the majority of the Bible is read completely over a period of time. (It takes two years if it is read during weekdays and three years if it is read only on Sundays.)

Lectionaries are used by Roman Catholic, Methodist and Church of Ireland churches, although they each have their own version. Those who use a lectionary argue that it is helpful and important as it ensures that the Bible is read systematically and that parts are not ignored.

Those churches which do not use a lectionary believe they should be free to read whatever part of the Bible they wish, according to how the Holy Spirit leads them.

The use of prayer in worship

The style of prayer used in worship ranges from formal, prepared prayers to unprepared, spontaneous prayers and even ecstatic or emotional prayers. Most churches will use one style more frequently than the others but this does not prevent them from using a combination of these types of prayer during worship.

The content of prayers also varies greatly and can depend on the church, the time of year and many other factors. However, it is possible to categorise some of the main purposes of prayer:
1. **Praise** – a prayer in which Christians express adoration to God.
2. **Confession** – a prayer in which Christians admit they have sinned and ask for forgiveness.
3. **Thanksgiving** – a prayer in which Christians thank God for what he has done in their lives.
4. **Petition** – a prayer in which Christians ask God for what they need in their lives.
5. **Intercession** – a prayer in which Christians pray for the needs of other people.

There can also be differences in the posture used by Christians when praying. Some churches encourage a variety of postures including sitting, standing and kneeling, while in other churches the worshippers will always adopt the same pose of bowing their heads and closing their eyes.

Worship as a way of life

Many Christians believe that worship is not just something which is done on a Sunday or in church. They believe that it is important to show adoration, obedience and devotion to God through their actions and behaviour every day.

For some Christians this may mean joining a religious community and making a special commitment to live a life of devotion, prayer and service. For the majority of Christians, living a life of worship involves a constant struggle to follow the example of Jesus and the commands of the Bible in everything they do and say.

Activity 1

Read the following statements by Christians of different backgrounds. In pairs, discuss how each one tries to live their life as a way of worship.

Statement 1

Daphne Shilliday is a member of the Church of Ireland.

> As a believing Christian I try to follow Christ's teaching. I am a teacher in the kindergarten Sunday School. I sing in the church choir and I also visit two elderly members of our parish. I work three days a week in a café and enjoy meeting people and, where possible, share my faith. My husband died almost three years ago from cancer and I know I could not have got through this without my faith and the many who prayed for us.

Statement 2

Noreen Kennedy describes herself as a believing Christian and attends a Presbyterian church in east Belfast.

> I find that the Sunday service, especially the worship and the sermon, help to set me up for the week ahead.
>
> By reading the Bible and using daily Bible notes, I am able to sustain my faith. Having two young children I don't have the time I previously had for prayer and Bible study but during the day, for example, while travelling to work in the car, I am able to pray. I am also a member of a home group and a prayer triplet. The home group involves about 14 people from our church who meet fortnightly for prayer and Bible study. The prayer triplet is where three people meet each month to share experiences and pray for each other.

Statement 3

Sister Margaret is a member of a Dominican religious order.

> There are two main ways in which I live my life as a sign of worship to God.
>
> The first way is through actual worship, for example prayer. This is community prayer, which includes morning prayers, evening prayers, night prayers and others. Personal prayer takes the form of daily meditation, as well as reading the Scriptures and other spiritual books. I also participate in the Eucharist.
>
> The second way is through active ministry. This means different things for different people. It may involve areas of education, family and parish ministry, social work and action for justice. Some of the things I'm involved in are working with refugees by teaching English to asylum seekers and working with the deaf children of travellers.

Plan some questions of your own on worship to ask people from some of the denominations you will be studying in this unit. Think about what exactly you would like to know and phrase your questions carefully in order to get a specific answer. Share the results with the rest of the class. You might also report back on some of the following:

a) What was the most interesting thing you discovered?

b) Were you surprised by any of the answers?

c) Did the opinions of the individuals seem to be similar or different to what you might know of others in their denomination?

Activity 2

Using the information in this chapter, organise a balloon debate.

Each person in the class is asked to represent one of the four main styles of worship outlined at the start of this chapter and make notes for a speech to defend their views. Four members of the class, each representing one of the main styles of worship, are asked to enter the basket of the balloon by coming to the front of the class. They must then make a speech and try to argue their case. Once everyone has spoken, the class must vote to choose one person to be thrown out of the balloon. Those remaining must give another speech defending their ideas.

The process of speaking and voting continues until there is only one person left in the balloon – the winner! (Obviously you can repeat the activity using four other members of the class.)

WORSHIP IN THE BAPTIST CHURCH

Activity

Read the following statement which was written by a Baptist pastor from Belfast. In pairs, discuss the questions which follow.

Generally speaking, Baptist churches do not use a written liturgy. While the format of services may be broadly similar from week to week, prayers are usually offered extemporarily . . . Congregational singing forms an important part of any Baptist meeting and prayer meetings are occasions when people are free to contribute as they feel they should. There is a sense of everyone having an opportunity to contribute to the spiritual life of the church even though leadership and preaching roles are quite clearly defined.

Pastor David McMillan,
A Tapestry of Beliefs, p 110

From reading this, what impression do you get of how Baptists regard worship?

Can you pick out any particular words or phrases which are important?

Clive Johnston from Magherafelt Baptist explains that they use a mixture of formal and informal styles of worship during their services:

A blend of formal and informal worship helps believers, especially older ones, to feel secure, while the more informal approach appeals to young people. It is important to be relevant and sensitive to all ages and backgrounds.

An overview of weekly worship

The majority of Baptist churches hold different meetings throughout the week which give them an opportunity to worship. The weekly activity sheet for Magherafelt Baptist Church below shows details of how their members worship.

The Sunday service

The main Sunday service in the Baptist Church usually takes place in the morning and includes two parts, a time of **Family Worship** and the **Breaking of Bread** or communion.

As there is no set pattern for Sunday worship in the Baptist Church, each individual church has the freedom to structure its worship in whatever way it chooses, but most services will include some or all of the ingredients on the next page.

DAY	WORSHIP ACTIVITY
Sunday	Sunday School and Bible Class, 10.00 am
	Morning service, 11.30 am, followed by a celebration of the Lord's Supper
	Family service, 4.30 pm, once a month
	Evening Service, 6.30 pm
Monday	Baptist Women's Fellowship, 8.00 pm
Wednesday	Ladies' Study of Scripture, 10.00 am
	Lunchtime Study of Scripture, 1.00–2.00 pm
	Church Prayer Meeting, 8.00 pm
Thursday	Divorce Care, 8.00 pm

- **Welcome and announcements** – these may be published on an information sheet.
- **Prayer** – pastor may ask someone to lead in prayer from the floor.
- **Hymns and choruses**.
- **Children's talk** and children's hymn – may be given by the pastor or a member of the congregation.
- **Bible readings** – sometimes read by a member of the congregation.
- **Sermon** – given by the pastor, this is the longest part of the service. Baptists believe that through the Bible readings and the sermon they are listening to God's word.
- **Communion** (follows the main service).

Susan, a member of a Baptist church in County Londonderry, explains what she enjoys about Sunday worship:

Attending Sunday worship at my local Baptist church gives me an opportunity to meet with other believers under the Spirit of God for fellowship, guidance and encouragement.

I enjoy the relaxed atmosphere of worship created through the singing and the informal style of the sermon. I find that by participating in the worship I am spiritually edified and prepared for the week ahead. The pastor is able to relate God's word to me as an individual and he addresses the problems young people face in today's world.

The Bible

The *Baptist Confession of Faith* states that, "The Holy Scripture is the only sufficient, certain, and infallible rule of all saving knowledge, faith, and obedience".

Baptists, therefore, give the Bible the highest priority in worship, believing that it is more important to hear what God has to say to them than what they have to say to him.

There is no lectionary in a Baptist Church, but Bible readings are a central part of Baptist worship. The pastor will generally choose readings which follow a theme that is then taken up in his sermon.

Members of the congregation, including young people, may do the Bible readings on a Sunday and all members of the congregation can be involved in discussing passages from the Bible during midweek Bible studies.

The version of the Bible used in the Baptist Church varies from church to church. In some, the Authorised Version is still used while others have moved to the New King James. In Magherafelt Baptist the New International Version is used because they believe it is best suited across the age ranges, although there is no problem with individuals following a different version if that is their preference.

Prayer

Most prayers during a Sunday service are spoken by a pastor in his own words. When worshippers meet during the week for a special prayer meeting it is also usual for each person to pray in a **spontaneous** way. Baptists tend not to use set prayers, such as the Lord's Prayer. Occasionally during a Sunday service, a pastor or member of the congregation may read prayers from a book, but this varies from church to church.

Baptists use different types of prayer during worship. For example, the first prayer in the morning service may be a prayer of adoration, focusing the thoughts of the congregation on who God is and what he is like, as well as their response to that.

In the middle of the service in Magherafelt Baptist an offering is taken and this provides a time for the congregation to think about everything God has given them, through prayers of thanksgiving.

This is also a time when they bring to God the needs of the church, their community, their country and the world.

Other forms of praise

As well as traditional **hymn singing**, the singing of modern **choruses** forms part of Baptist Church worship. Some Baptist churches, like Magherafelt Baptist, may have a **worship group** to accompany the singing. The younger members of the congregation tend to be more exuberant in their worship, clapping along with the more lively choruses.

Times of worship are not limited to the weekly Sunday services. For example, in Magherafelt Baptist there is a **Family Worship service** held once a month on a Sunday afternoon. And for the younger members of the congregation there is a monthly **youth rally**, called 'Lifeline', which welcomes people from any part of the community.

Questions

1. *How are members of the congregation involved in a Sunday service in the Baptist Church?*
2. *Using examples explain the importance of the Bible in the Baptist church.*
3. *What style of praying do Baptists prefer? What reasons might they give for choosing to pray in this way?*
4. *How do Baptist churches try to encourage young people to participate in worship?*

WORSHIP IN THE CHURCH OF IRELAND

Activity

Read the following extracts from the Revised Catechism of the Church of Ireland, a statement of its beliefs and practices. In pairs, discuss the questions which follow.

Q. What do we mean by the worship of God?

A. To worship God is to respond to his love, first by joining in the Church's offering of praise, thanksgiving and prayer, and by hearing his holy word; secondly by acknowledging him as the Lord of my life, and by doing my work for his honour and glory.

From reading this, what impression do you get of how Church of Ireland members regard worship? Can you pick out any particular words or phrases which say something important?

Worship in the Church of Ireland is mostly **liturgical** in style. Canon Stuart Lloyd explains why this is important:

I value a set liturgy. Many people like what they are familiar with, they know what is going to happen and they can relax and enter into the worship without worrying about what is going to happen next. Some people will disagree and say it is much the same every Sunday, but that does not mean it can't be valued. Presumably, if you like a particular piece of music you will want to listen to it again and again and really get into it.

I also see the liturgy as a drama in which we try to involve the congregation in all sorts of ways, we all have our parts to play and we respond to each other and there are different moods, like a drama.

Also from a clergyman's point of view a set liturgy is good, because worship then doesn't depend on how the minister is feeling or whether they are good or bad at particular aspects of worship.

Prayer books

Prayer books have a very significant part to play in worship in the Church of Ireland. Anglicans believe these provide a **structure** which helps worshippers express their thoughts to God. They also think they encourage all members of the congregation to be involved in the public act of prayer, uniting them in their devotion so that they feel part of the Christian family. Most congregations now use the *Alternative Prayer Book* although some still prefer the older *Book of Common Prayer*.

An overview of weekly worship

The number of services in a Church of Ireland church varies depending on the number of churches in a parish. There is normally a Holy Communion service held in most parishes each Sunday, as well as services for morning and evening prayer. During the festivals of Advent, Lent and Holy Week there are also special midweek services.

Activity

Read the paragraph below, in which Canon Lloyd describes the weekly worship in St Patrick's Church in Ballymena.

Design a poster for a notice board which might appear outside the church advertising the different services

Basically, on Wednesday morning there is communion every week; on a Sunday morning there is always an 8:15 Holy Communion service and always a service at 11:30 which is generally morning prayer, but once a month it is communion.

Once a month on Sunday morning at 10:00 there is a family service. In the evening there is always a service at 6:30 which is evening prayer, but once a month it is communion.

The Sunday service

An outline of Morning Prayer, when used as the main Sunday service, is as follows.

- **Greeting, welcome, hymn** and **prayers of confession**.

- **Ministry of the Word**: readings from the Old and New Testaments, canticles (scripture passages set to music) and the Apostles' Creed.

- **Prayers**: the Lord's Prayer, Collects (see below), prayers of intercession.

- **Hymn** and **sermon**.

- **Ending**: collection of the offering, a blessing and hymn.

The service is usually conducted by a minister of the Church of Ireland, but if communion is not celebrated, services can be taken by a **lay-reader** (a member of the congregation who has received training to assist at services or to preach if necessary).

Members of the congregation may also be involved in reading from the Bible or collecting the offering, if one is taken. All members of the congregation participate through singing, reciting creeds and saying prayers.

Lorraine, a member of a Church of Ireland in Fermanagh, explains the significance of Sunday worship to her:

One thing that worship does is help me to focus on God and his kingship. In a sense, it helps me to get things into perspective when I may feel things are getting out of control – worship reminds me that there is someone in control. Also I value the peace I get through worship, an inner peace and inner strength which fortifies me. There is a sense of belonging and of fellowship through worship which I find encouraging. and that can be a real help when facing the difficulties of life.

The Bible

The Scriptures are a central and essential element in the worship of the Church of Ireland.

During all services there are readings from the Bible which follow the pattern set out in their lectionary. Canon Lloyd feels a lectionary is important because, "it enables us to cover the broad spectrum of scripture and means we don't focus on only one particular aspect of the Bible."

Worshippers in the Church of Ireland also believe that the Bible has influenced and inspired all aspects of the liturgy contained in their prayer books. The sermon will usually be based on one of the Bible readings. Canon Lloyd believes the Bible is central to every part of worship in the Church of Ireland: "The liturgy is soaked in Scripture, virtually all the liturgy is based on Scripture and even many of the hymns we use have a scriptural basis."

Prayer

According to the *Revised Catechism of the Church of Ireland*:

Prayer is the uplifting of heart and mind to God. We adore him, we confess our sins and ask to be forgiven, we thank him, we pray for others and for ourselves, we listen to him and seek to know his will.

The majority of prayer in a Church of Ireland church is **liturgical** and read from books. In most cases it involves the worshippers by asking for responses at particular points. Canon Stuart Lloyd feels that this is the best way to pray in church:

Extempore prayer can be very meaningful and helpful but it has its difficulties, as it is dependent on whoever is leading it. With set forms of prayer this can be avoided. I very much value and enjoy reading the liturgy as I feel there is so much of value contained in every prayer and in every sentence we say. There is so much in it that you can never exhaust it, and so one tries continuously to let it speak in a fresh way.

Some of the main types of prayer include:

- **Collects** – short prayers with three parts: addressing God, a petition, asking to be heard (pleading) through Christ.

- **Prayers of Confession, Intercession, Thanksgiving** and **Praise**.

- **Private prayer**.

Posture during prayer is important to members of the Church of Ireland. At some points during worship they stand for prayer and at others they sit or kneel. Most churches provide stools for kneeling, but it is up to each individual to choose whether or not to kneel.

Other forms of praise

While Church of Ireland worship is mostly book-based there is still a great variety of worship which takes place. Canon Lloyd explains the many forms of praise which occur in St Patrick's, Ballymena:

In St Patrick's there is a strong choral tradition, but we also have a music group which plays at some special services and at our family service. It encourages a freer style of worship and, yes, it has been known for people to break into clapping even in the Church of Ireland. We have services when young people are to the fore. In all there is a great variety of worship in the Church of Ireland, from the quiet early communion service to the noisy family service, the gathering of a few in the evenings; from regular weekly services to the big occasions such as midnight communion on Christmas Eve and New Year.

Questions

1. **What are the main prayer books used in the Church of Ireland?**

2. **What style of worship is most common in the Church of Ireland?**

   What reasons might someone give for choosing to worship in this way?

3. **What is a lectionary?**

4. **How important is the use of the Bible in the Church of Ireland? Give reasons to support your opinion.**

5. **What postures do members of the Church of Ireland use during prayer?**

   How do you think changing posture might help worshippers during prayer?

A Collect for Peace

O God, the author of peace and lover of concord,
to know you is eternal life,
and to serve you is perfect freedom: } 1. Approach to God
Defend us in all assaults of our enemies, } 2. A Petition
that we, surely trusting in your protection,
may not fear the power of any adversaries;
through Jesus Christ our Lord. } 3. Pleading through Christ

WORSHIP IN THE METHODIST CHURCH

Activity

Read the following extracts from A Catechism for the use of the people called Methodists and in pairs discuss the questions which follow.

> Q. What is the worship of God?
>
> A. To worship is joyfully to proclaim, in the power of the Spirit, the wonderful acts of God and to celebrate his glorious nature. We worship God, not only in formal or informal acts of worship, but also with our lives, by serving him in serving other people.

From reading this, what impression do you get of how Methodist Church members regard worship? Can you pick out any particular words or phrases which say something important?

Worship in the Methodist Church is **structured** in style but can also include the reciting of creeds and prayers. The Reverend Heather Morris explains the importance of worship in Dundonald Methodist:

As we offer all that we are to God in worship there is a sense of his majesty, and we can be reminded by his Spirit of the privilege of being called to serve him and of the strength he promises. Christians can gain strength from God, the encouragement of the Holy Spirit, and his gifts. They can be reminded of their faith, and they can also gain insight and understanding. Fellowship is also a vital part of worship – fellowship with God and with one another. We come together, as his body, to worship God.

An overview of weekly worship

In the majority of Methodist churches there are two services on a Sunday, as well as midweek services for prayer and Bible study.

Activity

Read the paragraph below, in which Reverend Morris describes the weekly worship in Dundonald Methodist Church. Design a poster for a noticeboard that might appear outside the church advertising the different services:

> There are two services on a Sunday, one at 11.00 am and the second at 7.00 pm. Holy Communion is celebrated at least once a month as part of the Sunday morning or evening service.
>
> The church aims to provide opportunities for Bible study for all who are interested. There is a meeting for Bible study each Tuesday evening, and a Bible study for people ages 25–35 which meets every Monday.
>
> The Youth Fellowship meets every Sunday night after the evening service. This is for young people from age 11 to 18. Their activities include Bible study, teaching and worship along with fun-based activities. Members of the Youth Fellowship have developed strong relationships with one another and they support each other in every aspect of their lives, including their faith.
>
> A young adults' group also meets for fellowship, discussion of moral and ethical issues and worship and Bible study. Wedding and funeral services are also held.

The Sunday service

The structure of worship on Sundays can vary from church to church. In some cases there is a regular structure which follows the liturgy contained in the *Methodist Service Book*. However, it is more common for services to change from week to week and to include mostly free forms of worship.

Usually, in both cases, the service will include three main parts: **preparation**; **ministry of the word**; and **response**. The form of the Sunday service also depends on whether it is a family service or a communion service. Communion is usually held once a month. A Sunday service in a Methodist church that does not include the Lord's Supper (another term for communion) usually comprises the following principal parts:

Preparation:	Call to worship Hymns focusing on the nature of God Prayers of adoration and confession.
Ministry of the Word:	Hymns Readings from the Bible A sermon A creed
Response:	Prayers of thanksgiving The offering Prayers of intercession and petition The Lord's Prayer Hymn and dismissal

Glenda, a member of a Methodist church in Fivemiletown, explains why she enjoys Sunday worship:

It is lovely to meet with other people in a combined spirit of worship; people of all ages worshipping God together. Worship through the medium of music and song forms a very important part of our church tradition. We sing a combination of old- and new-style hymns and songs – I particularly enjoy this aspect of Sunday worship. Some of the service is structured in a liturgical style – I find this beneficial in that the entire congregation can follow and meditate upon the words. I also feel Sunday worship sets you up for the week ahead. We can come across all sorts of circumstances and situations from day to day, some happy, some sad, some challenging or difficult. In these situations a line of a prayer, a line of a song or a hymn, a verse of scripture or something said in the sermon will come to mind and encourage at such times.

The Bible

The Bible plays an important part in the worship of the Methodist Church as well as in the lives of individual members. This is symbolised by an open Bible being placed on the communion table.

Methodist churches use a lectionary based on the Old and New Testament Scriptures, so the Bible is read regularly in Sunday services and the sermon is usually based on a specific Bible passage. The Bible is also used indirectly through the saying of creeds and prayers contained in the *Methodist Service Book*. Methodists believe these are based on the Bible.

The importance of the Bible is also seen in the fact that members of the church gather in small groups during the week to study it. Reverend Morris says:

The Bible is seen as being central in belief and as a guide for life. Through reading and studying the Bible the Holy Spirit can lead Christians to deeper maturity, and indeed can lead people to faith.

Prayer

The *Methodist Catechism* gives six different forms of prayer:

1. **Adoration** – to praise and worship God.

2. **Confession** – to come to God and say sorry.

3. **Intercession** – to pray for others.

4. **Petition** – to pray about your own needs and concerns.

5. **Thanksgiving** – to thank God for all that he has done.

6. **Meditation** – to reflect quietly and wait for God to speak.

During a Sunday service prayers may be recited, such as the Lord's Prayer, read by the minister or spoken freely without preparation (extemporaneously). On some occasions in Dundonald Methodist Church they also use music, visual images or silence to help focus their minds during prayer.

Prayer in the Methodist Church is also more than something that is done on a Sunday. The Reverend Morris explains:

Prayer is also regarded as being vital and is integral to the life of the church. There is a prayer meeting on a Thursday morning, the Bible study ends with prayer, and there is a prayer chain where individuals can phone prayer requests to a prayer coordinator who passes that request on to others.

We have just started a monthly newsletter so that members of the congregation can be informed as to church activities but also so that they can pray in an informed way about all that is happening.

Occasionally specific services of prayer for healing are held. We do this in obedience to the scriptural commands to pray and in the belief that God asks his people to bring their requests to him, and also because of the belief and experience that God answers prayer.

Other forms of praise

There is a type of service which is unique to the Methodist Church called a **covenant service**. This service is held once a year – usually at the beginning of each New Year – and is a time when members of the Methodist Church reflect on their faith and recommit themselves to God through a renewal of their covenant.

Some Methodist churches may occasionally have special types of worship service, such as youth services, although in Dundonald Methodist Church they have developed a policy of making all of their services inclusive and varied.

There is a strong tradition of singing in the Methodist Church. Charles Wesley, one of the founders of Methodism, wrote over 7,000 hymns, many of which are still used in Christian churches today.

Questions

1. What are the three principle parts of a Sunday service in most Methodist churches?
2. Using examples, explain the importance of the Bible in Methodist worship.
3. Give three examples of how prayer could be used in the public or private worship of Methodist Christians.
4. What is a covenant service and what reasons might a member of the Methodist church give for choosing to attend such a service?

Glengormley Methodist Youth Choir in full voice.

WORSHIP IN THE PRESBYTERIAN CHURCH

Activity

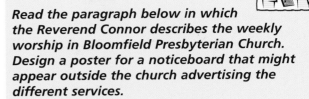

Read the following extract from The Directory of Public Worship *which is used by the Presbyterian Church in Ireland. In pairs, discuss the questions which follow.*

When the congregation is to meet for public worship, the people (having before prepared their hearts thereunto) ought all to come and join therein; not absenting themselves from the public ordinance through negligence, or upon pretence of private meetings.

Let all enter the assembly, not irreverently, but in a grave and seemly manner, taking their seats or places without adoration, or bowing themselves towards one place or other.

The congregation being assembled, the minister, after solemn calling on them to the worshipping of the great name of God, is to begin with prayer.

1. **From this, what impression do you get of how Presbyterians regard worship?**
2. **Can you pick out any particular words or phrases which are important?**

The Reverend Graham Connor explains the style of worship in Bloomfield Presbyterian Church in Belfast:

I would describe our worship as free, but we wouldn't get up and do things off the top of our heads; there is a theme to it but there is not a set liturgy. It is also God-centred.

So many people today say "I want to go to a church that satisfies my needs", but the main reason we should worship is to honour God.

We don't surprise people in our order of the service, but there is variety from week to week. It has a traditional feel to it, but there are also modern aspects too, such as drama and lively singing.

An overview of weekly worship

Activity

Read the paragraph below in which the Reverend Connor describes the weekly worship in Bloomfield Presbyterian Church. Design a poster for a noticeboard that might appear outside the church advertising the different services.

We have two main worship services on a Sunday, one at 11:30 in the morning and the other at 7.00 at night. During the week we have a service on Wednesday and home groups. The midweek service is a Bible study, discussion and prayer time; the home groups are occasions when church members meet in each other's homes for prayer and Bible study.

They are building blocks for fellowship – a congregation of this size is difficult to hold together, so when new people come along we introduce them to a home group and they get to know 10 or 12 other people and start to feel at home.

The Sunday service

The main Sunday service is led by an ordained minister, who always takes responsibility for the sermon. Members of the congregation collect the offering and may do some of the Bible readings or prayers, but generally the minister carries out the majority of the duties, as Reverend Connor explains:

Many of the people, men and women, young and old in the church would be asked to participate in church worship, from leading worship to saying prayers and doing readings. There might also be a drama or soloists.

The service may vary considerably from church to church, but the main ingredients are listed on the next page.

A Sunday morning service in Bloomfield Presbyterian Church would usually take one hour and a quarter, with the majority of the

- A call to worship
- Singing
- Prayers of confession

} Approach to God

- A children's address
- Singing
- Readings
- Prayers of adoration and praise
- A sermon

} Proclamation of the Word

- A collection and prayers of intercession
- Singing
- A blessing and dismissal

} Response to the Word

time (20–30 minutes) devoted to the sermon. The sermon would be an exposition of the Bible readings, that is, it would involve an explanation of the text and attempt to apply it to the present day.

Colin Jellie, a member of a Presbyterian church in Lisburn, explains what Sunday worship means to him:

Sunday worship is a chance for me to spend time in the fellowship of other Christians giving thanks to God. Our church makes an effort to cater for a wide age range – for example, there is a varied mix of traditional and more modern hymns used.

Worship helps me to appreciate what God has done within my life and provides time for reflection and being in God's presence.

In particular I like the prayers of intercession when we think of the sick and those needing help. I think it is good to take time to collectively remember these people.

Sunday worship also provides me with a break from my usually busy way of life. I receive a feeling of happiness as I am thanking God for all that he has provided.

The sermon section of Sunday worship gives me spiritual strength and helps me to focus on striving to do God's work and seeking forgiveness for my wrongdoings.

The Bible

Presbyterians regard the use of the Bible as central to their worship because it is God's word. This does not mean that God himself wrote the words contained in the Bible but that he inspired individuals to write the Bible. When a minister reads from the Bible and explains the meaning of it to their congregation, each person can understand something about God from it.

The significance of the Bible in worship is underlined by the fact that when a Sunday service is about to begin, an elder will place an open Bible in the pulpit as a symbol that the congregation are now about to listen to the Word of God. There are also Bibles in the pews so that everyone can follow the readings and, if necessary, refer to the Bible during the service. Presbyterians believe that people should be able to open the Bible and, with the help of the Holy Spirit, understand it for themselves. However, the minister is usually considered to be the best interpreter of the Bible, because of his education and training.

Prayer

The *Larger Catechism* of the Presbyterian Church offers an explanation of prayer. It states that, "Prayer is an offering up of our desires unto God, in the name of Christ, by the help of his Spirit; with confession of our sins, and thankful acknowledgment of his mercies." It also offers some guidance about who to pray for, what to pray about and how to pray:

Who should a Christian pray for? The Church, people in authority, ourselves, our friends, fellow Christians and even for enemies. A Christian must not, however, pray for the dead.

What things should a Christian pray for? For others, for themselves, and for anything which glorifies God. Christians must not pray for anything which is unlawful.

The interior of Bloomfield Presbyterian Church.

How should a Christian pray? A Christian must pray with a sense of their own insignificance, sinfulness and unworthiness in comparison to the greatness and holiness of God. They should be thankful, humble and serious when praying but also loving, eager and trusting in the way they speak to God.

During the Sunday service, the midweek service and at any other time prayer is usually **extemporaneous**, although from time to time if a member of the congregation is leading the prayer, they may prefer to prepare the words beforehand.

During the midweek meeting there is usually a time of open prayer, when anyone can contribute. Reverend Connor explains what happens in Bloomfield Presbyterian Church:

Generally speaking there would be a time of thanksgiving and adoration, but the majority of the time would be given to intercession, which would include prayer for situations in our congregation, situations in the wider community and situations in overseas mission which we have links with, such as Japan and Nigeria.

Many Presbyterian churches also encourage their congregations to organise prayer groups which can meet informally in people's homes to share concerns and pray together.

Other forms of praise

In the Presbyterian Church, **psalms** are sung as well as **hymns**. The psalms are the Scottish Metrical psalms, that is, translations of the Old Testament book of Psalms, but in verse form to make them easy to put to music. If you visit a Presbyterian church you may notice the hymn boards at the front which display a selection of hymns and psalms to be sung during a service.

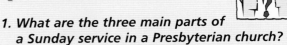

Questions

1. **What are the three main parts of a Sunday service in a Presbyterian church?**

2. **How might members of the congregation be involved in a Sunday service in the Presbyterian Church?**

3. **How important is the use of the Bible in Presbyterian worship? Give examples to support your opinion.**

4. **Using examples, explain the significance of prayer in the worship of a Presbyterian church.**

WORSHIP IN THE ROMAN CATHOLIC CHURCH

Activity

Read the following extracts from the Catechism of the Catholic Church, a statement of Catholic beliefs and practices. In pairs, discuss the questions which follow.

The Liturgy is the summit towards which the activity of the Church is directed; it is also the fount from which all her power flows.

para 1074

You cannot pray at home as at church, where there is a great multitude, where exclamations are cried out to God as from one great heart, and where there is something more: the union of minds, the accord of souls, the bond of charity, the prayers of the priests.

St John Chrysostom, para 2179

From reading this, what impression do you get of how Catholics regard worship? Can you pick out any words or phrases which are important?

An overview of weekly worship

In St Oliver Plunkett's Church there is a variety of worship activities which take place through the week, including formal services of Mass and informal Bible study and prayer groups. Father Dallat comments:

Each weekday we have Mass at 9.00 am. The Tuesday Mass also incorporates a Perpetual Novena to Our Lady. On Saturday we have Mass at 10.00 am and 7.30 pm and confession is from 6.30 pm to 7.30 pm. On Sunday there is one main service at 12.00 noon.

There are also scripture groups and prayer groups in our parish, although these are not formal services. A small number of the congregation meet on a Wednesday night to study the Bible together and we have prayer groups, including charismatic prayer groups who meet once a week and more traditional Rosary groups who meet before or after Mass to say the rosary together. House groups are also encouraged at Advent and Lent.

Activity

Read Father Dallat's description of weekly worship in St Oliver Plunkett's Church . Design a noticeboard to advertise the worship activities which take place each week at this church.

The Sunday service

The main Sunday service is called the **Mass** and in some churches there are four or five Masses said each Sunday. There is a common structure for every Mass and a priest of the Catholic Church must always lead it. The service will vary from week to week depending on the church calendar, the music used, the decoration of the church and the contribution made by members of the congregation, but the basic order remains the same.

1. **Introductory rites** – the priest welcomes the congregation and together they confess their sin and pray for forgiveness.

2. **Liturgy of the Word** – readings are made from the Old and New Testaments and a short sermon or **homily** is given. The **Nicene Creed** is recited and prayers of petition are said.

3. **Liturgy of the Eucharist** – a collection is taken and the bread and wine are prepared for Holy Communion. These 'gifts' are prayed over and offered to God. There is then a Eucharistic prayer during which the bread and wine are blessed, followed by the Lord's Prayer and the **Sign of Peace**, when people shake hands and greet one another with the words 'peace be with you'. The congregation now comes forward to the altar rail to receive communion. When they return to their seats there is a time of silence and reflection and possibly a hymn or piece of music followed by a prayer.

4. **Concluding rite** – a final blessing and prayer are said before the priest dismisses the congregation by saying, "The Mass is ended, go in peace." Music is played or a hymn is sung as the priest leaves and the service ends.

John, a member of a Catholic church in Belfast, explains the importance of Sunday worship for him:

> For me the most important part of Sunday Mass is the coming together as a community to hear the word of God, in particular, stories of Jesus' life which we can apply to our everyday lives.
>
> I enjoy the use of music in Sunday Mass and I think even more significance could be placed on it. Music adds joy and energy into the Mass; it encourages people and gives them hope. It can also be used for prayer and reflection, helping the people to come together as one voice to praise God.
>
> In general, I would say that Sunday Mass is a foundation, it brings things into perspective. If things have been troubling me during the week they seem to fade away on reflection and help me to start the week fresh and more prepared for anything I may face in the following week.

The Bible

The Scriptures play a central and essential element in the liturgy of the Catholic Church.

At Sunday Mass there is a reading from the Old Testament, a psalm from the Book of Psalms, a New Testament reading (Acts or Letters) and a reading from the Gospel. Each reading is selected according to the lectionary cycle of the church.

As well as the direct reading of the Scriptures, there are references to Biblical passages in the prayers and creeds recited during worship and the homily may contain a reflection on a particular reading.

Prayer

The *Catechism of the Catholic Church* states that there are five basic forms of Christian prayer:

1. **Blessing and adoration** – when Christians acknowledge the greatness of God.

2. **Petition** – involves pleading and asking God for forgiveness and help with everyday needs.

3. **Intercession** – asking on behalf of another.

4. **Thanksgiving** – showing appreciation for God's gifts in every aspect of life.

5. **Praise** – giving glory to God, not for anything he has done, but simply because of who he is.

These various types of prayer are used in the Catholic tradition on different occasions and in different ways. For example, some may be used during Holy Communion, as part of private prayer or while saying the **Rosary**. The Rosary is a repetitive type of prayer or chant which can be used in private or in public. The worshipper often uses beads when saying the Rosary to keep count of the prayers said. The structure of the Rosary comprises a short series of introductory prayers and then reflections on the three **Mysteries**.

1. **The Joyful Mysteries:** the annunciation; Mary's visit to Elizabeth; the Nativity; the presentation of Jesus in the temple; the finding of the boy Jesus in the temple.

2. **The Sorrowful Mysteries:** the agony in the garden; the scourging at the pillar; the crowning with thorns; the carrying of the cross.

3. **The Glorious Mysteries:** the resurrection; the ascension; the descent of the Holy Spirit at Pentecost; the Assumption; the coronation of our lady as the Queen of Heaven.

For each Mystery, a person recites the 'Our Father', ten 'Hail Marys' and one 'Glory Be to the Father'. You can read these on the next page.

THE HAIL MARY

"Hail Mary full of Grace, the Lord is with thee. Blessed art thou among women and blessed is the fruit of thy womb Jesus. Holy Mary Mother of God, pray for us sinners now and at the hour of our death. Amen."

THE GLORY BE TO THE FATHER

"Glory be to the Father and to the Son and to the Holy Spirit. As it was in the beginning is now, and ever shall be, world without end. Amen."

Other forms of praise

Within the structure of the Mass it is still possible for there to be a great variation in the styles of worship in a Catholic church. At some services there may be very traditional **choirs** who sing in Latin and with four-part harmonies, but you also have **folk masses** which are more lively and try to appeal to the younger people through the use of a range of folk instruments such as guitars and violins.

The style of folk masses varies greatly from church to church, depending on the musicians and instruments available.

Questions

1. **What are the four principal parts of a Catholic Mass?**
2. **How might the style of worship in a Catholic Church be described?**
3. **How might a service vary from week to week?**
4. **Using examples, explain the importance of prayer in Catholic worship.**
5. **Give three examples of how the Bible is used in a Catholic Mass.**

The interior of St Oliver Plunkett's Roman Catholic Church, Toomebridge.

END OF UNIT REVIEW

End of unit questions

1. Choose any three of the following and explain how and why they are included in some acts of worship:
   - *Readings from the Bible*
   - *Communion*
   - *Hymn singing*
   - *Prayer*
   - *Sermon/homily*
   - *Reciting the Apostles' Creed*

2. Describe some key differences in the Sunday act of worship in two different denominations.

3. Why do some denominations like to use the same style of worship each Sunday? What are the advantages and disadvantages of this?

4. Choose two of the following types of prayer and explain how they can be used in a worship service:
   - *Confession*
   - *Intercession*
   - *Petition*
   - *Adoration*
   - *Thanksgiving*

5. Some people think that church worship, especially the music, needs to change to appeal to younger people.

   How do you think it could be made more meaningful for:
   - children of primary age?
   - teenagers?

Activity

Feelings and Faith

a) *In groups or as a class try to think of different ways in which people can express their feelings creatively.*

b) *Try to look at examples of how some people have expressed their feelings about their faith through music, art or drama. (You could use some of the pictures in this book.)*

c) *Working with one or two others, design a piece of music, write a poem or a letter or perform a piece of drama which expresses your own feelings on one of the themes below.*
   - *God*
   - *Thankfulness*
   - *Confusion*
   - *Anger*
   - *Love*
   - *Peace*

Learning outcomes

As a result of studying of this unit you should:
- *understand what worship means;*
- *know about key aspects of worship in two traditions;*
- *examine how differences in worship reflect differences in religious belief.*

Tips for exam success

Always read a question several times before you attempt to answer it.

Write out some of the questions above and underline the key words which tell you what it is you have to do.

In pairs, discuss what you think each question is asking.

Sacraments and ordinances

4

INTRODUCTION

Throughout history, Christians have found it difficult to agree about what sacraments are, how many there should be and what happens when you take part in a sacrament. There is probably no definition of a sacrament that would satisfy all Christian traditions, but one image sometimes used to describe a sacrament is that of **a channel to and from God**. In particular, it is a way in which God can give his blessing or grace to Christians and they can show their obedience and devotion to God. Sacraments are associated with the performance of particular rites or ceremonies such as **baptism**, **communion** or **confirmation**.

Few or many?

The Roman Catholic Church believes there are seven sacraments whereas most Protestant Churches believe there are just two; the Baptist Church prefers to call them **ordinances**. The Salvation Army and Quakers have none.

A source of grace or a symbol?

The Presbyterian, Methodist, Church of Ireland and Roman Catholic churches feel that when a sacramental ceremony takes place, God's grace is given to the person receiving the sacrament.

However, each of these churches understands the idea of God's blessing in a slightly different way. Roman Catholics believe that grace is given to an individual at a specific moment during the ceremony whereas Presbyterians believe that grace is received in a more general way.

For other churches, such as the Baptist, sacraments are merely symbols and, while they do offer an opportunity for a believer to draw nearer to God in faith, they do not impart God's grace as a direct result. That is why some denominations prefer the term 'ordinance' rather than 'sacrament'.

Baptism

Infant or Believer's Baptism?

There is a long tradition in Christianity of baptising babies and infants but during the Reformation in the sixteenth century some Christians challenged this practice, saying that it is not mentioned in the Bible. These were known as **Anabaptists** (literally 're-baptisers') and they believed that a person should be baptised only after being converted to Christ as a result of a personal decision. The Baptist, Brethren and some other evangelical churches continue to hold this belief today.

Those who baptise infants admit that there is no direct mention of infant baptism in the Bible, but they maintain that their tradition is based on several Biblical examples which mention whole families being baptised. They say that in these cases there is no suggestion that children or infants were excluded, therefore it must be permissible.

On the other side, those who baptise only believers argue that the Bible contains many examples of believer's baptism and so it is clear that this is the correct and logical way of baptising people, as faith in God is a personal decision which must be made before baptism can take place.

Activity

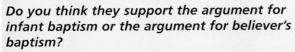

Look up these Bible references.

Do you think they support the argument for infant baptism or the argument for believer's baptism?

Acts 2: 38–41

Acts 8: 35–39

Acts 16: 13–15, 31–34

Acts 18: 8

Sprinkling or full immersion?

There are three main ways which have been used to baptise people in the Christian tradition: **sprinkling with water** from a person's hand; **pouring water over the head** using a jug or by standing beneath running water; and **full immersion**, where the body and head of the candidate are put fully under water, for example in a river or pool.

Those who baptise infants generally acknowledge that immersion is one way of baptising, but there are other ways including sprinkling and pouring which have been carried out for many years.

Baptists and others who practise believer's baptism argue that immersion is the only acceptable form of baptism. They explain that the word which is translated in the Bible as 'baptism' is the Greek word *baptizo*, which literally means to plunge, dip or immerse. They also point to a passage in Paul's letter to the Romans where he is talking about baptism and uses the symbolic image of death, burial and resurrection. This, they say, is clearly a reference to immersion during baptism.

The requirement for believing parents

For those churches who practise infant baptism there is often a question of whether a minister or priest should automatically agree to baptise the children of all parents who request it, or whether certain conditions should be set so that a parent or parents can prove that the vows they take on behalf of the child will be taken seriously. In the majority of Presbyterian churches, for example, it

is necessary that at least one parent is a baptised member of the church and that they regularly attend Sunday worship.

The situation can vary from church to church, even within one denomination. Some churches set very specific conditions. Others are much more relaxed and believe that if the parents show a desire for the child to be baptised, the minister or priest should not decide who should or should not receive God's grace.

Eucharist/Communion

In the majority of Christian churches celebration of the Eucharist holds a place of great importance. Different churches refer to it by different names such as **Holy Communion**, the **Lord's Supper**, the **breaking of bread** and the **Mass**. The term Eucharist is normally used by teachers or academics when talking about this sacrament in a general way, but when discussing the celebration of the Eucharist in a particular church it is best to use the title which that church prefers. For example, Anglicans prefer Holy Communion whereas Baptists prefer the Lord's Supper. The word Eucharist is a Greek word meaning 'thanksgiving' which tells us two things about this sacrament.

1. At the Eucharist, Christians are **remembering** the Last Supper of Christ when, on the night before he died, he gave thanks for bread and wine before sharing it with his disciples.

2. By participating in the Eucharist, Christians are **expressing their thanks** to God.

The foundation and inspiration of this sacrament is found in the Bible, and it usually involves the blessing of bread and wine (sometimes called **elements** or **signs**) which the congregation then eat. However, each church chooses to celebrate the sacrament in its own way.

The reason they do things differently is because they each have their own beliefs and ideas about the meaning and importance of the sacrament. We will look at some of the main issues over which there is disagreement.

Real presence or symbol?

During a service of the Eucharist does the bread and wine merely represent the body and blood of Christ in a symbolic way or are they changed in a special way so that Christ becomes actually present in the elements? And if Christ's real presence is in the elements does the bread actually become his body and the wine his blood or does his presence co-exist with the bread and wine?

Activity

Read John 6:48–58 and discuss what it might mean for Christians and their understanding of what happens during the Eucharist.

Sacrifice or memorial?

Christians believe that Christ's death was so important because, by dying, he was offering himself to God as a sacrifice to take away people's sin, in the same way that Jews used to offer animals to please God. When Christians take part in a Eucharist service some believe they are simply remembering the death of Christ and the sacrifice which he made.

Others believe that the Eucharist is a type of sacrifice during which Christ's body and blood are offered up on an altar in the same way that he was crucified. In this case, the congregation are actually participating in the death of Christ.

Frequent or seldom?

Some argue that because the Eucharist is the single most important act in the life of the church it cannot be celebrated often enough, and some churches will offer communion at least once a day.

Other churches argue that because it is such a holy and significant sacrament that it must not be abused in any way and so people must not become over-familiar with it. They should celebrate communion only four or five times a year and should take time to prepare properly in their hearts and minds before each occasion.

One kind or both kinds?

During the 15th century it became compulsory for Roman Catholics to receive only the bread at the Mass. The reasons were mostly practical – the danger of spilling the blood of Christ, the time taken to administer the cup to large numbers, and the issues of hygiene which arose from all sharing one cup. In all other churches which celebrate the Eucharist it is taken in both kinds, bread and wine. The Roman Catholic Church does now permit communion of both kinds to take place, but it is still more common to receive the bread alone.

Preserve or throw away?

What happens to the leftover bread and wine after the service depends on whether the church believes in the real presence of Christ in the bread and wine. If they do they will not want Christ to be mistreated in any way and so the bread and wine is either completely consumed or it is kept in a special place, to be used again.

For those Christians who believe that the bread is merely a symbol and never becomes anything other than bread, they are quite at ease with disposing of the bread and wine in a normal way.

All welcome or members only?

Some churches, like the Baptists, invite anyone who has made a commitment to Jesus Christ as their Saviour and Lord to receive communion. Others, such as the Roman Catholic Church, say that it is only those who are baptised members of the church who can participate, nor should members of their church receive communion in any other.

These are just a few of the divisive issues regarding the Eucharist. Others include:
• whether the wine should be drunk from a single cup or individual cups,
    • whether the wine should be alcoholic or non-alcoholic
    • whether the bread should be in the form of wafers, shortbread or a loaf.

Activity

1. *Read 1 Corinthians 11:28–29. Explain how these verses might be used by a Christian who believes that the Eucharist should be celebrated only occasionally.*

2. *Read Acts 2:42–47. Explain how these verses might be used by a Christian who believes that the Eucharist should be celebrated frequently.*

3. *What is your opinion on how often Christians should celebrate the Eucharist?*

Confirmation

For churches which practise infant baptism, confirmation is a further stage of admission into the church. In this instance an individual repeats their baptismal vows, confirming that they are willing to take upon themselves the promises made for them by their parents when they were babies. In this way an individual becomes a **full member** of a church. For many young people, confirmation is considered a milestone in their development and the event is often accompanied by a family celebration.

There is no mention of a ceremony of confirmation in the Bible, but those who practise it believe that there are good reasons for its use. The Roman Catholic Church, for example, believes that the tradition of the **laying on of hands** in the New Testament church is the origin of the sacrament of confirmation.

Activity

Look up Acts 2:1–4 and comment on how this might be used by those who believe that a type of confirmation existed in the early church.

Like the other sacraments and ordinances mentioned above, there are several key issues relating to the practices and beliefs surrounding confirmation.

Age of confirmation?

There are different views on when a person should be confirmed or become a full member of a church. The typical age of confirmation in the Roman Catholic Church is ten whereas in the Church of Ireland confirmation is usually carried out in the teenage years. The key issue is the age at which a person really understands the commitment they are making.

Before or after first communion?

Some argue that the most important part of the process of initiation into the church is baptism, and once that has taken place a child or young person should be permitted to take communion and feel a full part of the worshipping community. Others argue that a child is not ready to take communion until they have participated in the special preparation that is part of confirmation and which allows them to understand fully what it is they are doing.

A special blessing from the Holy Spirit or a public statement?

Roman Catholics believe that confirmation is a sacrament. During the ceremony there is a moment when the participant is blessed by God in a special way. It is believed they receive the mark or the seal of the Holy Spirit which gives encouragement and strength to each Christian to live a life in the service of God.

Protestants do not regard confirmation as a sacrament but, in general, see it as a time for decision making, when people come to a mature understanding of what it is to be a full member of the church and commit themselves to this.

Activity

For discussion

1. *Do you think it is a good idea to have a ceremony to mark the beginning of adult responsibility, when a young person feels ready?*

2. *At what age do you think a young person is ready to make a decision about their religious commitment?*

ORDINANCES IN THE BAPTIST CHURCH

Baptists, in general, prefer not to use the word sacrament when referring to baptism and communion. They do not believe that there is any special power or presence of God during these ceremonies in their churches, and so they prefer to call them **ordinances**. Pastor Clive Johnston explains:

> An ordinance is something that Jesus ordained or appointed for his church to strengthen believers. Baptists see an ordinance as a visual aid of gospel truth, given by Christ to strengthen our faith and also to affirm or renew our allegiance to Jesus as our Saviour and Lord.

Baptism

Who is baptised?

Baptists do not baptise infants; they believe that only those old enough to understand what is happening to them should be baptised, and only after they have made a personal commitment to Jesus Christ as their Lord and Saviour. This is why the type of baptism practised in the Baptist Church is often referred to as **believer's baptism**. Children as young as eight or nine years of age can be baptised, but it is usual for young Christians to wait until they are of secondary school age before they take the step.

Method of baptism

Believer's baptism is by **total immersion**. Baptists believe this was the method used in New Testament times (see Matthew 3:16; Acts 8:38; Romans 6:1–14). They also point out that the Greek word *baptizo* used in these texts means 'to dip' or to 'submerge'.

A ceremony of baptism

Baptism in the Baptist Church always takes place in public as it is regarded as a kind of announcement, or confession, of faith as well as a chance to witness to those who do not share the same beliefs. It is also a way for the local church to welcome publicly the newly baptised individuals into membership of the local church.

A ceremony of baptism usually takes place as part of a Sunday service at which the Lord's Supper is not celebrated, and normally at the end of a service, as this gives the pastor and those being baptised an opportunity to get changed and ready.

The routine may vary from church to church but usually contains the following parts:

- The baptismal tank is opened and the pastor, dressed in a shirt and trousers, will descend into the tank which is filled waist deep with water.

- The person being baptised will then follow the pastor into the water. Men usually dress in a white shirt and dark trousers while women wear a special baptismal robe.

- The pastor will ask the person: "Do you now confess Jesus Christ as your Lord and Saviour?" The candidate answers, "I do." This may be extended to allow the person being baptised to give some details about their conversion experience.

- The person being baptised clasps their hands in front of their chest. The pastor places one of his hands on the person's hands and the other behind their back.

- The pastor then says, "On profession of your faith in the Lord Jesus Christ as your personal Saviour, I now baptise you in the name of the Father and of the Son and of the Holy Spirit. Amen."

- The pastor then plunges the person under the water until they are fully immersed, and then quickly brings them back up to a standing position.

- The newly baptised individual then makes their way up the steps of the baptismal tank to get dried and changed into other clothes.

- A hymn is sung and the service may be followed by a short celebration of the Lord's Supper.

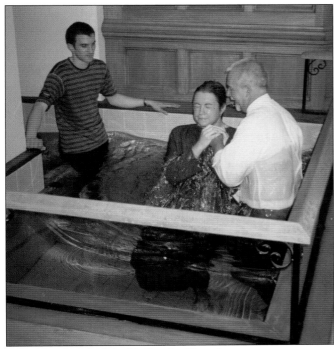

A baptism in Magherafelt Baptist Church.

In the Baptist Church the candidate is given a **Certificate of Baptism** which gives details of the date of baptism, the name of the candidate, the name of the pastor who performed the baptism, and the title of the local congregation.

Beliefs about baptism

Look at the following statements from the *Baptist Confession of Faith*:

Baptism is an ordinance of the New Testament, ordained by Jesus Christ, to be unto the party baptised, a sign of his fellowship with him, in his death and resurrection; of his being engrafted into him; of remission of sins; and of giving up into God, through Jesus Christ, to live and walk in newness of life.

Immersion, or dipping of the person in water, is necessary to the due administration of this ordinance.

Things Most Surely Believed Among Us, The Baptist Confession of Faith, with Scripture Proofs, of 1689

From this we can conclude:
- Baptists baptise because Jesus commanded it (Matthew 28:19–20).
- Baptists consider baptism to be an outward expression of an inner faith.
- Baptism by immersion is a symbol of the death, burial and resurrection of Christ as well as a visual representation of the change which has taken place in the individual who, in becoming a Christian, has left behind their old ways and experienced a **second birth** into a new kind of life.
- Baptism is also a means of formalising a person's faith and of accepting him or her as a member of the church.

The Lord's Supper

Who takes communion?

Baptists call communion the **Lord's Supper** and have what they call an **open table**, which means that anyone who has accepted Jesus Christ as their Saviour and Lord is free to participate in the ceremony whatever their age or background – you do not have to be a Baptist to take communion in a Baptist church. Pastor Clive Johnston explains:

Concerning the taking of communion, it's not how old you are but who you are. Whenever we celebrate the Lord's Supper, all those who know and love the Lord Jesus Christ as their personal Saviour are invited to share in the fellowship meal. So from the time a person becomes a Christian they are welcome to take communion.

How often is communion celebrated in the Baptist Church?

The Lord's Supper is celebrated every Sunday, at the end of the morning service. Baptists believe this is the practice of the New Testament (Acts 2:46; 20:7). In some churches there is an evening celebration of the Lord's Supper on the first Sunday of every month.

A ceremony of the Lord's Supper

Activity

Look at the description of a ceremony of the Lord's Supper in a Baptist church. Use the information to design an order of service which could be given to someone attending the church for the first time.

After the morning worship service, a proportion of the congregation leaves and there is a period of quietness. Then the pastor invites those gathered to share in the service.

There is a time of open worship when those present are free to choose a hymn or chorus, which everyone sings together. Someone might read a passage of Scripture, pray or even share something that would focus the thoughts of everyone on Jesus' death, burial and resurrection.

After this period someone would give thanks for the bread. The pastor then takes the plates of bread and gives them out to the deacons. One of the deacons serves the pastor with the bread. Sometimes they wait until everyone has a piece of bread and the congregation eat it together. Usually the deacons pass it around the congregation first and when they return to the front the pastor in turn serves them. The same procedure is followed for the wine.

Then, after a period of quiet, the pastor prays and announces the benediction.

Different Baptist churches may vary slightly in the order or way in which this is carried out. The Lord's Supper is a very informal time of sharing. Clive Johnson explains that this does not take away from the seriousness of it and in fact "everyone has something to add to it and it is a very enriching experience". The fellowship of believers takes place in the visible act of communion together.

Beliefs about the Lord's Supper

Baptists believe that in celebrating the Lord's Supper they are:

a) obeying Christ. St Paul records in the Bible that at his Last Supper Jesus commanded his followers, "Do this in remembrance of me" (1 Corinthians 11:24). Baptists believe that by participating in the 'breaking of bread' they are showing obedience to Christ. The *Baptist Confession of Faith* (1689) states therefore, that "The Supper of the Lord Jesus Christ was instituted by him the same night wherein he was betrayed, to be observed in his churches, unto the end of the world".

b) remembering Christ. By calling to mind what he did for them by dying on the cross. The bread and wine are signs and symbols of his body and blood. "In this ordinance Christ is not offered up to his Father . . . but only a memorial of that one offering up of himself by himself upon the cross, once for all" (*The Baptist Confession of Faith, 1689*).

c) identifying with Christ in his death and resurrection. They believe that their own conversion to Christianity involved a death of the old sinful person and a spiritual re-birth or resurrection. Taking part in the Lord's Supper, therefore, is regarded as "a bond and pledge of their communion with him, and with each other" (*The Baptist Confession of Faith, 1689*).

d) believing in Christ. By remembering Christ's sacrifice on the cross they are telling everyone that they believe Christ died for all and through his death they can be saved.

e) looking forward to Christ's return. Through the Lord's Supper Baptists "proclaim the Lord's death until he comes".

Church members at worship.

Admission into full membership of the Baptist Church

Baptism is important because it is an expression of a person's individual salvation. However, the importance of being part of the **family of God** is also stressed. To become a member of the Baptist Church it is necessary that a person:

- professes faith in Jesus Christ and repentance of their sins;

- shows a life transformed by the power of Christ;

- is baptised by immersion upon the profession of their faith;

- agrees with the doctrine of the Baptist Church.

In practice a person applies in writing and is interviewed by two elders who listen to their **testimony**, the story of how they became a Christian. A report of the interview is made at a special meeting of the church. The application must be approved by a two-thirds majority vote of those present. The person is then publicly received into membership at a meeting of the church, usually on a Sunday at the Lord's Table. The pastor gives the person the **right hand of fellowship** (Galatians 2:9) which is a sign that they are accepted into the fellowship of the church and are willing to commit themselves to the church.

Questions

1. **What is an ordinance?**

2. **Why is baptism in the Baptist Church often called 'Believer's Baptism'?**

3. **Why do Baptists believe that it is important for those being baptised to be fully immersed in water?**

4. **What do Baptists mean by saying they have an 'open table' at the service of the Lord's Supper?**

5. **Explain the process whereby a person is formally admitted into membership of a Baptist church.**

 # SACRAMENTS IN THE CHURCH OF IRELAND

The Church of Ireland *Revised Catechism* states:

. . . a Sacrament is the use of material things as signs and pledges of God's grace, and as a means by which we receive his gifts. The two parts of a sacrament are the outward and visible sign, and the inward and spiritual grace.

The Church of Ireland believes that there are only **two** sacraments: **baptism** and **Holy Communion**, although there are other **'ministries of grace'** which include confirmation, ordination, holy matrimony, the ministry of absolution and the ministry of healing.

Baptism

Who is baptised?

The most common form of baptism in the Church of Ireland is **infant baptism**, although adults who wish to join the church and have not previously been baptised may also receive the sacrament. It is also traditional to baptise by pouring water three times over the head of the child or adult. The reason why infants are baptised is explained by Canon Lloyd:

It would seem from Scripture that children were baptised and it was part of the Jewish tradition that children would be considered part of the people of God through the act of circumcision. Also Jesus placed a strong emphasis on the importance of children, and his acceptance of them would encourage me to think that the grace of baptism should not be kept from children.

A ceremony of baptism

Baptism nearly always takes place in public as the ceremony marks the welcoming of the child into the family of the church, and so it is appropriate that the church family is present.

A typical ceremony follows the pattern set out in the *Alternative Prayer Book*:

1. The introduction.
2. The ministry of the word.
3. The ministry of the sacrament:

(a) The decision: the parents are asked to answer three questions. Do you turn to Christ? Do you renounce the Devil and all his works? Will you obey and serve Christ?

(b) At the font: the water is blessed.

(c) The baptism: the parents are asked to affirm the Apostles' Creed. Then the minister takes the baby, pours water over its head and says "__, I baptise you in the Name of the Father and of the Son and of the Holy Spirit." The minister also makes the sign of the cross on the baby's forehead before the whole congregation welcomes the child into the family of God by saying:

God has adopted you by baptism into his church. We therefore receive you into the household of faith, as a member of the body of Christ, as the child of the same heavenly Father, and as an inheritor with us of the kingdom of God.

Everyone then recites the Lord's Prayer.

After a baptism the child will receive a **baptismal card** which is an official record that the ceremony has taken place.

Beliefs about baptism

Baptism in the Church of Ireland is understood as a gift from God. The *Revised Catechism* states that this gift is "union with Christ in his death and resurrection, the forgiveness of sins, and a new birth into God's family". In other words baptism is understood as a two-way process:

1. **What God gives**: membership of Christ and his body, the church; forgiveness and new life.
2. **What the person brings**: repentance and faith.

Baptism in the Church of Ireland is also described as the start of a journey in the Christian life which requires a personal commitment from each child when they are old enough to understand the promises which have been made on their behalf. As Canon Lloyd comments, "Baptism is about becoming one of Christ's, but the person must respond to that, must unwrap the gift, take it for themselves and make it their own."

Holy Communion

Who takes communion?

A person normally takes communion for the first time at confirmation, around 14 or 15 years old, although it is not required for a person to be confirmed to take communion. In some Church of Ireland churches there is a trend to allow participation in the Holy Communion at an earlier age and to delay confirmation to a later age. Normally a child who does not take communion will still come forward to the altar rails during the distribution of bread and wine in order to receive a blessing.

Beliefs about communion

The Church of Ireland teaches that during a service of communion the worshippers remember, celebrate and anticipate.
1. They **remember** the suffering and death of Christ.
2. They **celebrate** his resurrection and ascension
3. They **anticipate** the coming of God's kingdom.

When taking communion, members of the Church of Ireland believe that to the faithful, Christ is really present in the bread and wine in a spiritual way, and that the elements are sacred. The *Revised Catechism* states that: "Receiving the Body and Blood of Christ means receiving the life of Christ himself." (See panel opposite)

Confirmation

The age of confirmation tends to be 14 or 15, although it can be at any age after this. Confirmation is carried out by the bishop.

A service of Holy Communion in the Church of Ireland

- The preparation
- A greeting
- A preparation prayer (a collect for purity)
- An act of praise (generally the 'Gloria in Excelsis')
- The ministry of the word
- Readings from the Bible by laypeople
- Sermon
- A response to the word of God in the form of the Apostles' Creed
- Prayers of Intercession, usually led by laypeople, which follow a set form as well as allowing the individual an opportunity to contribute.
- Reading of the commandments
- Confession
- Absolution
- Prayer of humble access
- The peace (the form can vary – shaking of hands, exchange of greetings etc)
- The offertory – usually a hymn is sung while the offering from the congregation is collected. The collection is then brought forward to the altar and the bread and wine are also placed there.
- The ministry of the sacrament

There are four actions which make up the ministry of the sacrament – taking, blessing, breaking and giving.

(i) The minister takes the bread and wine into his hands.

(ii) The bread and wine are blessed and the minister makes a long prayer of thanksgiving which ends with the whole congregation saying the Lord's Prayer

(iii) The minister breaks the bread and says, "The bread which we break is a sharing in the body of Christ." The congregation replies, "We, being many, are one body for we all share in the one bread."

(iv) The minister gives the bread and wine to the people. Members of the congregation walk forward, a row at a time, to the altar rail at the front of the church where they kneel and cup their hands to receive the bread and take a sip from a goblet of wine when it is offered to them by the minister. During the distribution of bread and wine the minister repeats the words: "The body of Christ keep you in eternal life," "The blood of Christ keep you in eternal life." Laypeople may act as assistants to help with administering the cup or the bread.

- After communion

After every one has participated in receiving the bread and wine there is a giving of thanks and a prayer of commitment to serve Christ. The service ends with a blessing and the minister says "Go in peace to love and serve the Lord." The congregation replies "In the name of Christ. Amen."

Preparation

Before a person is confirmed they attend **confirmation classes** where they learn about the tradition, teaching and worship of their. One programme used with young people at these classes is called the 'Archbishop's Challenge' which is a resource pack of fact sheets and activities to help young people learn in a more interesting way.

At the end of the classes a person is then ready to take their confirmation vows, having learnt the significance of what they are about to do.

Order of a confirmation service:

1. Introduction

2. Readings

3. Bishop's address (homily)

4. Renewal of baptismal vows during which young people are asked if they will lead a life that is committed to Christ

5. Prayer for the seven-fold gifts of the Spirit

6. Those being confirmed come forward to the bishop and he lays his hands upon them

[over]

7. Prayer of confirmation

8. Holy communion – the newly confirmed people receive communion with their families and members of the congregation.

After the confirmation the occasion is usually concluded by a cup of tea in the parish hall, when those being confirmed have an opportunity to meet the bishop. Some families will also have a special celebration at home.

Beliefs about confirmation

The Church of Ireland believes that confirmation is a serious moment in the life of an individual, taking, as they do, the promises of baptism upon themselves. It is also an opportunity for the church to say to the young person that they are valued and have a place in their local church.

However, Anglicans believe that being confirmed is very different from joining a club because by being confirmed three important things take place.

1. A person is confirmed by the Holy Spirit and strengthened to live a Christian life.

2. A person is confirmed by the bishop in their Christian faith.

3. A person confirms their own baptismal promises.

Questions

1. **How many sacraments are there in the Church of Ireland and what are they?**

2. **Why do baptisms generally take place in public?**

3. **In what way can baptism in the Church of Ireland be described as a two-way process?**

4. **Explain what happens during the four actions of the sacrament of Holy Communion – taking, blessing, breaking and giving.**

5. **How do young people in the Church of Ireland prepare for confirmation?**

6. **What is the religious significance of the ceremony of confirmation?**

SACRAMENTS IN THE METHODIST CHURCH

Methodists recognise **two** sacraments: **baptism** and **Holy Communion**. While they practise confirmation they do not regard it as a sacrament. John Wesley, the founder of Methodism, defined a sacrament in the words of the Church of England Catechism: "an outward sign of inward grace, and means whereby we receive the same".

Baptism

Who is baptised?

Methodists believe that infants should be baptised as a way of welcoming them into the church. The Reverend Heather Morris explains: "Baptism signifies incorporation into the body of Christ, a sign that the child is loved by God and is part of the family of God's people."

The practice of infant baptism does not exclude the baptism of older children or adults and there are outlines for such services in the *Methodist Service Book*. We will look at the most typical ceremony, which would involve an infant.

A ceremony of baptism

The baptismal service usually occurs during a Sunday morning service, emphasising the symbolism of the child becoming part of the whole church. At a point during the service the parents and sponsors (sometimes known as **godparents**) are invited to bring the child to the baptismal font, which is usually at the front of a Methodist church. The ceremony then follows the order set out in the *Methodist Service Book*:

1. The Bible is read.

2. The congregation make a promise that "they will so maintain the common life of worship and service that he/she and all the children among you may grow in grace and in the

knowledge and love of God and of his Son Jesus Christ".

3. The parents make promises to teach and guide the child in Christian ways.

4. The minister asks the parents to announce the child's name.

5. The minister pours or sprinkles water over the child's head and says, "__, I baptise you in the Name of the Father, and of the Son and of the Holy Spirit."

6. The child is often given a Bible.

7. The minister leads the congregation in prayer for the child and their family.

Beliefs about baptism

Underlying the practice of infant baptism is the Methodist belief in the power of God's grace, that God gives his love to people whether or not they deserve it and, in the case of infants, even before they are aware of it.

While baptism is a very important part of the life of a Christian, Methodists believe that it is possible to be a Christian without being baptised. Rev Heather Morris explains:

Being a Christian is based on a personal decision to surrender everything into God's hands and receive Jesus as Saviour. However, baptism is a sign and seal of membership of the church.

Communion

Who takes communion?

At a service in a Methodist church everyone present is invited to participate. The traditional invitation to the Lord's Table is "to those who love Him or who would like to love Him more". John Wesley encouraged Methodists to receive the Lord's Supper as often as possible.

Traditionally a young person receives communion after they have been received as a full member at a reception service (see page 86). However, children who are not full members will often come to the communion table and be blessed.

A service of Holy Communion in the Methodist Church

A communion service is held in Methodist churches at least once every month. Normally it is held during a Sunday morning or evening service, but can also be celebrated in a more informal way with small groups or even outside the church building. It is vital, however, that an ordained minister be present. A typical communion service held during a Sunday service would take the following format.

1. The service begins with preparation and the ministry of the word, and prayers for others.

2. The **Nicene Creed** may be said together as a sign of unity with other parts of the body of Christ. There is a time for sharing the peace.

3. The bread and wine are on the communion table, covered with a cloth. They are then uncovered and the congregation say a prayer of thanksgiving. Significant elements in this prayer are:

– praise
– remembering: this prayer rehearses the way in which Jesus inaugurated the Last Supper
– thanksgiving
– recognition of joining with "all the company of heaven" through worship
– looking forward to Christ's coming again
– obedience: celebrating communion in obedience to Christ's command.

4. The minister then breaks the bread in the sight of the people, and invites them to come forward to the communion table where they kneel to receive. The stewards help the minister to distribute the elements.

5. When all have been served, the elements are covered, the people return to their seats and there are final prayers, perhaps a hymn and the benediction.

Beliefs about communion

The *Catechism* of the Methodist Church states:

> In the Lord's Supper Jesus Christ is present with his worshipping people and gives himself to them as their Lord and Saviour. As they eat the bread and drink the wine, through the power of the Holy Spirit they receive him by faith and with thanksgiving. They give thanks with the whole Church for Christ's sacrifice of himself once and for all on the cross. The Lord's Supper recalls Christ's Last Supper with the disciples. It proclaims Christ's passion, death and resurrection, unites the participants with him so that they are a living sacrifice in him, and gives them a foretaste of his heavenly banquet.
>
> *Catechism for the use of the people called Methodists, no. 49*

From this we can see that the celebration of communion is important to Methodists for several reasons:

1. By taking the bread and wine worshippers receive Christ's presence in a special way.

2. It is a way of giving thanks to God.

3. It reminds worshippers of the suffering and death of Christ.

4. It celebrates the resurrection and looks forward to the future when Christians will be with Christ in heaven.

Confirmation

Who is confirmed?

Once a child is old enough, he or she is encouraged to participate in the life of the church by attending Sunday School and church services, as well as joining youth organisations.

It is hoped that eventually the child will come to a point when they make a personal profession of faith, when they agree to live by the promises contained in their baptismal vows. This profession of faith is usually associated with a ceremony of confirmation, which takes place at a reception service. Reverend Heather Morris:

> Traditionally, confirmation does not take place before a young person is 14 or 15. At this point they are regarded as being mature enough to make their own decisions and to recognise the significance of this service. There is no upper age limit and as people come to faith and desire to commit themselves to the Lord and to the church publicly, they may be received at any age. So, for example, in Dundonald Methodist Church we have services of reception into full membership at which people of many ages will become full members.

Before a person can be confirmed in the Methodist Church they must participate in a **preparation course**, usually led by the local minister. The classes involve instruction and discussion about the Christian life as well as learning about the Methodist Church and the responsibilities of a full church member.

A service of reception

The reception service is always held in the context of a service of Holy Communion and follows the format set out in the *Methodist Service Book*.

- **The ministry of the word**: the Scripture passages describe the old covenant made with God's people and the new covenant written in the heart and fulfilled in Jesus. There is a reminder that Jesus calls people to follow him and that the Holy Spirit will help those being confirmed to keep the promises that they are about to make.

- **The promises and profession of faith**: here individuals confess their own faith in Jesus.

- **The confirmation and reception**: two symbolic acts are included in this section.

  (a) The laying on of hands – used in the New Testament as a symbol of the gift of the Holy Spirit or commissioning for a special task.

  (b) The giving of the right hand of fellowship which expresses welcome into the human society of the church. Often it is a steward who takes part at this point.

- **The Lord's Supper**.

What is the significance of a reception service?

The reception service is usually considered a special moment in the life of a Christian. Methodists, however, do not believe that confirmation is a sacrament, as Reverend Morris explains:

> We do not believe that change takes place through the service in its own right. This is an opportunity for individuals to confirm their faith in God and their commitment to him. During the service we pray that the person will be blessed and that they will be established in the Holy Spirit.

Questions

1. *How many sacraments do Methodists have and what are they?*
2. *Why do Methodists believe they should baptise infants?*
3. *Who is permitted to take communion in the Methodist Church?*
4. *Explain why the celebration of communion is important to Methodists.*
5. *At what age are people confirmed in the Methodist Church?*
6. *What are the key elements of a service of reception in the Methodist Church?*

A view of the pews and roof beams in Dundonald Methodist Church.

SACRAMENTS IN THE PRESBYTERIAN CHURCH

The *Shorter Catechism* of the Presbyterian Church explains that, "A sacrament is an holy ordinance instituted by Christ; wherein, by sensible signs, Christ, and the benefits of the new covenant, are represented sealed, and applied to believers." This means that a sacrament is a promise from God (**a seal**) which is acted out in a visible way, for all to see (**a sign**).

The Presbyterian Church teaches that there are only **two** sacraments, **baptism** and the **Lord's Supper**, and that God is present in these sacraments in a special way. However, they believe that God is also present in other ways in the church and in the world.

Baptism

Who is baptised?

It is usual in the Presbyterian Church for infants to be baptised, although it is also possible for adults who come to faith at a later age to be baptised as well. The infants and adults are usually sprinkled with water and although baptism by immersion is acceptable, it happens rarely.

In the majority of Presbyterian churches parents must fulfil certain criteria before their children are baptised, otherwise the minister may refuse baptism. A leaflet on the baptism of children published by the Presbyterian Church states:

> Some people think that a child may be baptised even if parents are not regular church goers, or do not have real faith, or are not yet married. This is not so. Baptism belongs to the Christian Church, to practising Christians and their children.

A ceremony of baptism

Baptism will almost always take place in public and most commonly during a Sunday morning service. It imposes a responsibility on the parents who promise to bring their child up in the Christian faith by:

- praying for and with the child;
- teaching the child about Jesus both in the home and by bringing the child to church and Sunday School.

The vows

Two questions are put to the parents:

1. In presenting this child for baptism do you profess your faith in God as your Creator and Father, in Jesus Christ as your Lord and Saviour, and in the Holy Spirit as your Sanctifier and Guide?

2. Will you by God's help, provide a Christian home and bring up this child in the worship and teaching of the church, so that your child may come to know Jesus Christ as Lord and Saviour?

A question is then put to the congregation, emphasising the importance of their role:

Do you promise to do all in your power to provide warm Christian fellowship for this child, to give instruction, guidance and a good example to him/her, so that in cooperation with the parents he/she may later come to give their life to Jesus Christ as their Lord and Saviour?

The baptism

The minister then takes the child and, making the sign of the cross on the child's forehead, using water from the font, says, "In the name of the Father, the Son and the Holy Spirit, I baptise you [name of child]."

The declaration

"We now receive this child into the fellowship of the Church and promise so to order our congregational life that he/she may grow up in the knowledge and love of God."

The congregation then sings the **Aaronic Blessing** (Numbers 6:24–26): "The Lord bless you and keep you. The Lord make his face to shine upon you and be gracious unto you", as a way of welcoming the child into the church family.

Beliefs about baptism

Presbyterians understand the importance of baptism in two main ways.

1. **As part of God's covenant with his people.**
In the Jewish tradition male children are circumcised shortly after birth as a way of marking them as part of the wider Jewish family, and to fulfil the promise (covenant) which Abraham made with God. So Presbyterians believe that baptising an infant is a way of bringing a child into the family of God by promising to bring the child up as a Christian.

However, Reverend Connor points out that "the child needs to come to personal faith as they grow up, but we pray, expecting that within the covenant, God's grace will be working in that person's life".

2. **As a sign of grace, not evidence of faith.**
Reverend Connor states:

We are spiritually dead and we can't make ourselves alive; only God can do that. The fact that the baby is helpless and cannot choose to be baptised is a symbol of the fact that salvation is something God does to us.

Communion

Who takes communion?

Everyone in the congregation who has a personal relationship with God is invited to take communion. It is not necessary to be baptised or to be a full member of the Presbyterian Church.

There is a tradition of children not attending the communion, but when young people feel ready to participate they usually discuss the matter with their local minister.

Presbyterians also keep a record of who attends the communion services by giving out **communion tokens**. People bring the token with them to the service to indicate that they are present at the communion. It is a way of checking that those who have promised to be part of the church are regularly at the Lord's Supper. If people stop attending then the minister or an elder will go out and talk with them to see if there is a problem with their own personal faith or their life in the church. Communion tokens also provide the church with a registry of communicant members which is required, for example, when it comes to such events as voting for new elders.

How often is communion celebrated?

The number of times communion is celebrated each year varies from one Presbyterian church to another – it is usually between two and six times a year. This is to encourage people to think deeply about the seriousness of the sacrament.

A **pre-communion service** is also held on the Wednesday before Communion Sunday, to allow people to prepare themselves spiritually before receiving communion. It also provides an opportunity for new communicant members to be received into the church.

Beliefs about communion

The central theme is "Commemorating the Lord's Death until he comes", although Presbyterians regard the Lord's Supper as more than just a memorial service. They believe that for each person taking part (**communicant**) the service is a time of:

- **remembrance** – keeping in mind the death of Jesus.
- **thanksgiving** – giving praise for the death of Jesus.
- **communion** – meeting with Christ.
- **nourishment** – being spiritually built up.
- **testimony** – declaring in a public way that they follow Christ.
- **fellowship** – enjoying the company of the Christian family.
- **dedication** – renewing one's commitment to Christ.
- **expectation** – looking forward to Christ's return

(adapted from *Introducing The Lord's Supper*, Presbyterian Church in Ireland)

A service of Holy Communion in the Presbyterian Church

The service is very similar to a normal Sunday service, although the sermon is shorter and there is no children's address. The sacrament of the Lord's Supper follows the preaching and involves the following.

1. An opening prayer.
2. A reading, for example from 1 Corinthians 11: 23–25 or from the gospels, perhaps Matthew 26:27–29.
3. The actions: bread is blessed and distributed, wine is blessed and distributed. It is given by the minister to the elders who distribute it to the congregation. Then the minister serves the elders.
4. Prayer.
5. Hymn.
6. Benediction.

The wine used is usually non-alcoholic and served in small glasses which are carried to the people in their pews on a special tray. Similarly the bread, which can be either ordinary bread or shortbread, is carried on a plate which the elders pass around the congregation.

The Reverend Connor explains:

The bread and wine signify the body and blood of Jesus; we don't believe that they become the body and blood, but they are meant to remind us by word, by sight, by taste that Jesus gave up his life for us. God is present in all services, but in the communion service we sense his presence and receive his grace in a special way.

Confirmation

Confirmation is not a term normally used in the Presbyterian Church. The process whereby a person becomes a full member of a local church is referred to as the **reception** of a communicant, although it is possible to receive communion before being a full member of the church. There is no lower age limit for becoming a full member, but in general the youngest a person would become a member is their mid-teens and the norm is around 18.

A couple of months before each communion service is held, the minister invites anyone who is interested in becoming a full member of the church to speak with him or her. If a large number come forward they may be asked to attend a **preparation class**; otherwise the minister will talk with them on a one-to-one basis.

Preparation for reception as a communicant member involves learning what full membership of a local Presbyterian church involves, as well as a person having an opportunity to talk about their faith and how they might contribute to the life of the church, using their talents and abilities.

A reception of communicants service

Reverend Connor describes a typical service to receive new members into Bloomfield Presbyterian Church:

A service to receive new members takes place on the Wednesday night before a communion Sunday. The new members meet with the Kirk Session formally and an elder welcomes them into the church; another elder would pray for them. During the service they would be asked

questions concerning their faith, about their commitment to the church here and about their general life.

At a reception of communicants each new communicant makes the following vows:

Since Jesus Christ the Eternal Son of God dwells in me by the Holy Spirit I shall endeavour with his help:

- to be open to His will for my life.
- to live in fellowship with Him through daily prayer and Bible Study.
- to obey Him and honour Him in my daily life and to witness for Him by what I say and how I live.
- to be regular in attendance at worship and at the Lord's Table.
- to be active in the life and work of my own church, to be loyal to its leadership and to support it financially and in every other way I can play my full part in His mission to the world.

On the Sunday morning following the confirmation service the names of the new members would be read out at the Lord's Supper and formally received into the fellowship of the church.

Questions

1. In the Presbyterian Church what does it mean that a sacrament is a 'sign' and a 'seal'?

2. Why might a Presbyterian minister refuse to baptise an infant?

3. According to Presbyterians what is the significance of baptism?

4. What are communion tokens and why are they used?

5. How often do Presbyterian churches celebrate communion? What reason might they give for this?

6. Explain the significance for members of a Presbyterian church of participating in a service of communion.

7. What are the responsibilities of a communicant member of the Presbyterian Church?

SACRAMENTS IN THE ROMAN CATHOLIC CHURCH

Sacraments are central to the life of all Catholics; in the same way that there are natural stages to everyone's life, sacraments are understood to be the stages of the spiritual life. The Catholic Church teaches that there are **seven** sacraments which can be grouped into three categories, as shown in the table below. Each sacrament has a symbol associated with it.

Sacraments are of central importance to the Catholic Church for several reasons.

1. They believe all seven sacraments were **special gifts** given by Christ to his followers during his life on earth.
2. They have formed a part of the life and worship of the **Christian tradition** for thousands of years.
3. They confer **grace**. By participating in the sacrament the believer receives a special blessing of the Holy Spirit from Christ.

CATEGORY	SACRAMENT	SYMBOL
Sacraments of Christian initiation	Baptism Confirmation Eucharist	Sprinkling with water Laying on of hands Bread and wine
Sacraments of healing	Penance and Reconciliation Anointing of the Sick	Priest's assurance of God's forgiveness Anointing with oil
Sacraments at the service of communion and the mission of the faithful	Ordination/Holy Orders Marriage	Laying on of hands by bishop Giving and receiving of rings

Baptism

Who is baptised?

Catholics practise **infant baptism**, believing that it is important that a child of believing parents should be introduced into the Christian life as early as possible. Parents will usually meet with their local priest to discuss the baptism of their child so that they understand the significance of the ceremony and the importance of the promises that they will make on behalf of the child. They may attend a pre-baptismal course.

On the day of baptism the child will usually be accompanied by his or her parents and **godparents**. (Godparents are usually friends or relatives who act as witnesses at the baptism and promise to offer help and encouragement to the child in their religious development.) Other relatives and friends also attend.

Baptism is also available to adults who come to faith in Christ later in life. In this case there is a period of preparation for the ceremony, which usually takes place at Easter. It is also different from infant baptism because, in the case of adults, the baptismal ceremony is extended to include the sacraments of confirmation and first communion.

A ceremony of baptism

Baptisms do not take place at a public Sunday service of Mass, but rather the ceremony is **private**, with friends and family invited. The ceremony is highly symbolic and represents a journey into the Christian life. The stages of the journey take place in four parts of the church.

1. At the door – the child, parents and godparents are greeted and welcomed into the church.

2. At the ambo – here the word of God is read and the priest gives a short homily to those present. The prayers of the faithful follow and the infant is anointed with the oil of cathechumens. This is a symbol of strength, originally given to adults preparing for baptism to protect them from evil until they were baptised.

3. At the font – firstly the water is blessed, then the priest asks the parents and godparents to make vows on behalf of the child. These are:

Priest – Do you reject Satan and all his works and all his empty promises?

Parents – I do.

Priest – Do you believe in God the Father Almighty, creator of heaven and earth?

Parents – I do.

Priest – Do you believe in Jesus Christ, his only son, our Lord who was born of the Virgin Mary, was crucified, died, and was buried, rose from the dead, and is now seated at the right hand of the Father?

Parents – I do.

Priest – Do you believe in the Holy Spirit, the Holy Catholic Church, the communion of Saints, the forgiveness of sins, the Resurrection of the body and life everlasting?

Parents – I do. This is our faith. This is the faith of the Church. We are proud to profess it in Jesus Christ our Lord.

The priest then pours water over the child's head three times while saying "__, I baptise you in the name of the Father and of the Son and of the Holy Spirit." This is the actual moment that the sacrament takes effect on the life of the child and it is followed by three other symbolic acts.

a) An anointing with the **oil of chrism**. In Biblical times kings, queens and prophets were anointed to show they were being chosen, and in the baptismal ceremony it shows that each child has been chosen by God.

b) The clothing with a **white robe**. This shows that through baptism the child has been washed clean of original sin and is now clothed in the purity of Christ.

c) The lighting of **a candle**. Light is a strong symbol of new life and hope. The baptismal candle is lit from the Paschal candle, symbolising that the faith of the church is being passed on to the child. The priest says, "Receive the light of Christ . . . May he keep the flame of faith alive in his heart".

4. At the altar – the ceremony is concluded at the altar with the Lord's Prayer and three blessings: one for the mother, one for the father and one for the friends and family present.

Finishing at the altar is significant because it points the minds of the parents and godparents to the future when the child will hopefully complete their initiation into the church through taking their first communion and being confirmed.

Beliefs about baptism

Infant baptism is part of the tradition of the Catholic Church and is a way in which parents can give thanks to God for the gift of their child.

According to Catholic teaching, it also brings about several important changes in the life of the child.

1. **Forgiveness of sins**. "By baptism all sins are forgiven, original sin and all personal sins, as well as all punishment for sin." (*Catechism of the Catholic Church* (hereafter *CCC*), 1263)

2. **Adoption as a child of God**. A baptised Christian is "a partaker of the divine nature, member of Christ and co-heir with him, and a temple of the Holy Spirit". (*CCC*, 1265)

3. **Membership of the body of Christ**. "Baptism incorporates us into the Church. From the baptismal fonts is born the one People of God of the New Covenant." (*CCC*, 1267)

4. **Unity with other Christians**. Baptism is "the foundation of communion among all Christians". (*CCC*, 1271)

5. **Spiritual consecration**. "Baptism seals the Christian with the indelible spiritual mark [character] of his belonging to Christ." (*CCC*, 1272)

Once a child has been baptised they receive a baptismal certificate which is an official record of their baptism.

Communion

This sacrament has several names in the Catholic tradition including the **Mass**, **Holy Communion** and the **Eucharist**. The word 'Mass' comes from the Latin word meaning 'I send', because at the end of the service the people are sent out to serve Christ in the world.

Who takes the Eucharist?

The Eucharist is offered to baptised Catholics over the age of eight. Christians from other denominations are welcome to attend a Mass, but they are not allowed to take part in the actual sacrament by receiving consecrated bread from a priest.

Before a child takes communion for the first time they undergo a period of preparation. This is usually done through **religious education classes in Catholic primary schools**.

When a young person receives communion for the first time it is considered to be a very important occasion. The children dress up in special clothes, the boys generally wearing shirts and ties while the girls wear white dresses.

A young girl dressed for her First Communion.

How often is communion celebrated?

The Eucharist is part of the Mass which is held daily in the Catholic Church. Because of its importance, Catholics are encouraged to go to Mass at least once a week.

Ceremony of the Eucharist

The most important part of Catholic worship is the Eucharist, which takes place during the Mass. Before attending Mass many Catholics prepare themselves by attending confession or by reflecting on what they have done wrong in their lives.

During the Mass there are readings, prayers, a homily, the creed and the Liturgy of the Eucharist. For a more detailed outline of the Mass, refer back to the section on 'Worship in the Roman Catholic Church' (page 70).

The Liturgy of the Eucharist in the Catholic Church

Father Dallat describes what happens in his church in Toomebridge:

After the Liturgy of the word comes the Liturgy of the Eucharist. This includes prayers which have been with the church for over 1500 years, describing what Christ did on his last night with the apostles.

We pray for the Holy Spirit to change the gifts into the body and blood of Christ, and we pray that the Holy Spirit will make the gathered assembly into the body of the Christ.

We then move into the communion rite. The 'Our Father' is said together, expressing our desire to be part of the faithful disciples, and then we share the Eucharist.

When the bread and wine are consecrated at the Eucharist, Father Dallat says the following words:

[Over the bread]
Take this, all of you, and eat it: this is my body which will be given up for you.
[Over the wine]
Take this, all of you, and drink from it;
   this is the cup of my blood,
the blood of the new and everlasting covenant.
It will be shed for you and for all so that sins may be forgiven.
Do this in memory of me.

In the Catholic Church normally only the bread is given to the congregation. The bread is a thin wafer (called a **Host**) which is placed into the mouth or the hand of the communicant by the priest or Eucharistic minister. Each person says 'Amen' to the words 'The Body of Christ'.

Right at the end of Mass there is a commission to go and live in peace with the Lord. Father Dallat explains that although the worship is meant to be a thanksgiving for the previous week, it is also a preparation for what lies ahead.

Beliefs about communion

There are three ways in which this sacrament is significant.

1. Thanksgiving: the word Eucharist means 'thanksgiving' and by taking communion Catholics are saying thanks to God for his gift of salvation.

2. Memorial: during a Mass, Catholics are reminded of Christ's sacrificial death, but this is not just a recollection of past events. Through the words and actions of a Mass the events of Christ's death are acted out and made real, so "the Eucharist is also a sacrifice". (*CCC*, 1365)

3. Presence: In the Mass Christ is present, as Father Dallat comments:

When we share the Eucharist we do not believe the bread and wine are just symbols of the presence of Jesus, but we believe Jesus makes himself really present through the power of the Holy Spirit.

Confirmation

Who is confirmed?

Confirmation in the Catholic Church is usually for children who are ten to eleven years old. It is a sacrament in which both the church and Catholic schools have a role to play.

Pupils who attend Catholic schools are prepared for their confirmation as part of the religious education classes led by their teachers and local priests.

A ceremony of confirmation

A confirmation service usually takes place during a Sunday Mass, but it is special in several ways. Normally the local bishop is present and the extended family of those being confirmed come along to watch and will later help them celebrate the event.

The ceremony of confirmation occurs before the sacrament of the Eucharist and involves three main parts.

1. The renewal of baptismal vows – the child says the vows which were originally said by his or her parents when they were baptised.

2. The laying on of hands – the child being confirmed comes forward and kneels before the bishop who places his hands on their head. This is a symbolic way of blessing someone and calling on God to fill them with power and strength.

3. An anointing with Chrism – immediately after the laying on of hands the bishop makes a sign of the cross with the oil of Chrism on the forehead of the candidate while saying, "__, be sealed with the gift of the Holy Spirit." He will then tap the child on the cheek as a sign that he/she should be prepared to face hardship for the faith.

Beliefs about confirmation

Confirmation is the final part of a young person's initiation into full membership of the Catholic Church. It is seen as a fulfilment of the sacrament of baptism, when the candidate makes a personal commitment to Christianity.

It is also believed that at confirmation the Holy Spirit fills the individual in a special way to enable them to take on the challenges they will face in the Christian life. Father Dallat remarks:

> I believe that any child who is confirmed receives the gifts of the Holy Spirit; but for some children they are like Christmas presents which they put in the back of a wardrobe because they don't know how to use them, and it is only later in life that they have the maturity and ability to use them.

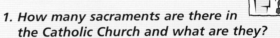

Questions

1. **How many sacraments are there in the Catholic Church and what are they?**

2. **What are the four key places in a ceremony of baptism in the Catholic Church? Briefly explain what happens in each place.**

3. **Explain the three ways in which celebrating the Eucharist is significant for Catholics.**

4. **What symbols and actions are associated with the sacrament of confirmation? Explain how each might make the ceremony meaningful for the person involved.**

END OF UNIT REVIEW

End of unit questions

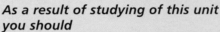

Baptism

1. Name a denomination which practises:

(a) believer's baptism;

(b) infant baptism.

2. Describe some of the differences between infant and believer's baptism.

3. Describe a baptismal ceremony from a denomination of your choice.

4. Name two symbols/actions which are used in baptism and explain their significance.

5. Explain why most baptisms take place in public.

6. "A minister should have the right to decide whether a person (adult or infant) is deserving of baptism."

    Evaluate this statement showing that you have considered more than one point of view.

Communion

1. Explain how communion/Eucharist is linked to events in the Bible.

2. Explain why communion/Eucharist is celebrated differently in two different denominations.

3. Outline a communion service in a denomination of your choice.

4. "Taking Holy Communion too often takes away from its importance." Discuss this question showing that you have considered more than one point of view.

Confirmation

1. Some young people are confirmed for the wrong reasons. Do you agree or disagree? Give reasons for your answer.

2. Confirmation is often followed by a party for friends and family. Do you think this is a good idea? Give reasons for your answer.

Activity

In groups, choose one sacrament in the Christian tradition you would like to learn more about. Try to find out and discuss traditions and practices in the celebration of the sacrament in different Christian churches around the world by making a link with pupils in another country. Your school may have an official link with other schools around the world; otherwise, a good place to begin is by looking at existing projects on the World-Links web-site (www.world-links.org/english). You may find one which you could join, or begin your own project and invite others to contribute.

Learning outcomes

As a result of studying of this unit you should

- understand the variety of meanings associated with the concept of sacrament;

- know about the practice of Eucharist/communion, baptism and confirmation in two traditions;

- understand some differences in Christian teaching on the sacraments of baptism, Eucharist/communion and confirmation.

- be able to express and justify a personal opinion about key controversies concerning sacraments.

Tips for exam success

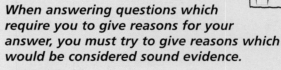

When answering questions which require you to give reasons for your answer, you must try to give reasons which would be considered sound evidence.

For example,

• use Biblical references

• refer to Church statements or documents

• mention specific well-known examples from history.

Try to avoid simply telling stories or merely giving a personal opinion. Make sure that your reasons are relevant. It would be a good idea to look at a variety of sample questions and discuss with your teacher what might be good evidence to consider for each one.

The role of the clergy and church leaders

INTRODUCTION

How many names or titles of leadership roles in different Christian churches can you think of? Do you know what jobs these different people do? I'm sure that if you try to answer these questions you will soon become surprised by the number of different titles and confused about the jobs they do.

The titles bishop, presbyter, elder, overseer and deacon all appear in the New Testament, which suggests that there were different types of leaders with different roles in the early church.

While some of these titles still remain, the jobs which bishops or deacons do now are very different from their previous roles.

Added to this confusing situation is the fact that different denominations today use many of the same titles, but they mean something different to each church.

Activity

Look at the following passages:

Philippians 1:1; 1 Timothy 3:1–8; Titus 1:5–7; 1 Peter 5:1–2.

1. **What names are given to the various roles people held in the early church?**

2. **Describe some of the qualities required to be a leader or helper in the church. Which of these do you think are still relevant today?**

As well as all the confusion about titles there are also strong differences of opinion within the Christian Church about who can be a leader, what special powers or attributes they have and even what they should wear.

Preacher or priest?

Most churches regard their main local leader (for example, pastor, minister or priest) to be a person who has special qualities and carries out special duties in the church, There are strong differences of opinion on what these qualities might be. A main difference is between those who see the function of their leader as primarily that of a teacher or preacher and those who see their leader as the person who celebrates the sacraments and therefore acts as an instrument through which God gives his grace to his people.

For example, Roman Catholics believe that priests have a very special role to play in worship because they are God's representatives:

> In the ecclesial service of the ordained minister, it is Christ himself who is present to his Church as Head of his Body, Shepherd of his flock, high priest of the redemptive sacrifice, Teacher of Truth. This is what the Church means by saying that the priest, by virtue of the Sacrament of Holy Orders, acts in persona Christi Capitis: 'It is the same priest, Christ Jesus, whose sacred person his minister truly represents. Now the minister . . . possesses the authority to act in the power and place of the person of Christ himself.
> *Catechism of the Catholic Church*, para 1548

The Presbyterian Church teaches that the minister does not have any special power or unique relationship with God, although they must have a gift for teaching and preaching because through the minister's preaching, God's word is communicated to the congregation: "They that are called to labour in the ministry of the word are to preach sound doctrine, diligently . . . plainly . . . faithfully . . . wisely . . . zealously [and] sincerely" (*Larger Catechism* A. 159).

Men or women?

Another controversial issue is whether women as well as men should be ministers, pastors and priests. The Methodist, Church of Ireland and Presbyterian Churches permit women in the ministry or priesthood of their churches, while the Roman Catholic and Baptist Churches do not. However, it is not possible to say that all Methodists, Presbyterians and Anglicans agree with the ordination of women, nor that all Roman Catholics or Baptists disapprove.

Those who disagree with the ordination of women use some of the following arguments to support their views.

- 1 Corinthians 14:33–35 and 1 Timothy 2:8–14 speak of the humble place women should have in the church.

- The twelve disciples of Jesus were men.

- The creation story (Genesis 1) shows that women were created as helpers to men.

Those who agree with the ordination of women use some of the following arguments to support their views.

- Galatians 3:26–27 says there is no difference between men and women – all are one in union with Christ Jesus. Therefore men and women are equal and should be treated as such by the Church.

- Jesus had a high regard for women and treated them with equality (see John 4:5–30; 8:1–11; Mark 14:3–9).

- If the church wants to reach out to men and women, then both sexes need to be represented in its leadership.

Special garments or plain clothes?

An issue which is certainly less important than the previous two, but which still causes strong differences of opinion, is whether ministers and priests should wear traditional garments which have a symbolic meaning or simply plain clothes.

Activity

Look at the following statements which give contrasting views on the importance of a cleric wearing special garments during worship. Make notes from these under the headings 'Reasons for ministers and priests wearing special garments' and 'Reasons for ministers and priests wearing plain clothes'.

We do not make a distinction between clergy and laity because we do not believe that this is found in the Scriptures. One of the basic beliefs we have is in the 'priesthood of all believers' (1 Peter 2:5&9; Revelation 5:10). Every individual has the ability to come right into the presence of God to pray without any mediator except Jesus, and they can worship and serve God. We do not see the role of pastor or minister as being separate from the people. Therefore we do not think you should wear special clothes.

Pastor Clive Johnston

The different clothes we wear at Mass may seem strange, outlandish and from a bygone time yet they do something to neutralise the person who is there, by playing down the personality of the priest. There is also something in the vestments which help us understand our history and where we come from. The over-colours are there as a visual reminder of the different seasons and feasts. When I put the garments on it is also to signify that I am doing something different and special. It is a way of saying that this is God's time.

Father Ciaran Dallat

Activity

1. *In groups, discuss the following statements.*

   (a) Men and women are equal in God's sight.

   (b) Men and women have different roles to play in church leadership.

2. *Now look at the arguments given above for and against the ordination of women. Using these arguments and any notes from your group discussion, write an essay or prepare a speech on the topic 'The Ordination of Women in the Christian Church'.*

KEY PERSONNEL IN THE BAPTIST CHURCH

In the Baptist denomination there is no single leader of a local church. The church is governed by a group of men called **elders**.

Elder

Elders are the spiritual leaders in the Baptist Church and are elected by the congregation they serve. They are required to be men of good character and show evidence of living a spiritual life. Elders can have different roles depending on their own abilities and training. The teaching elder is referred to as a **pastor** and, unlike the others, he has a full-time position in the church. One Baptist elder sees his place in the church as follows:

> I regard the role of an elder to be that of spiritual oversight. Jesus is the Good Shepherd and I have been entrusted with the role of an 'undershepherd', caring for the flock as well as sharing God's word with the flock.
> I find myself working alongside other elders with various responsibilities:
> – protecting the church members and adherents;
> – preaching God's word;
> – providing pastoral care (guidance, counsel, support, encouragement);
> – providing leadership for people.
> For me, being an elder is not about status or position, but rather an opportunity to serve God and others. It is an honour, a privilege and a responsibility which I take very seriously. It gives me a great sense of joy and fulfilment to serve in this role.

Pastor

Most Baptist churches in Ireland have one pastor. However, more churches are moving towards team ministry with several pastors who have different roles within the church, eg teaching pastor, assistant pastor/associate pastor, and youth pastor.

Training

There are no set requirements for training to be a Baptist pastor other than to be 'called' by a congregation. Probably around 50% of the Baptist pastors in Northern Ireland will have completed a course of study at the Irish Baptist College.

A pastor joining a church is formally accepted by the congregation at a service of induction. Here he is given **the right hand of fellowship** (a handshake) as a sign of his acceptance by the congregation.

Dress

Baptists do not make a distinction between clergy and laity and therefore do not believe it necessary for pastors to wear special clothes or a clerical collar.

Duties

Clive Johnston of Magherafelt Baptist Church explains that in his job as a pastor there is no such thing as a typical week. His duties include:
- mid-week Bible study and prayer time;
- sermon preparation: This is not simply two or three hours studying a passage of Scripture. Everything that happens during the week – my relationships with others, my reading on a wider scale, things that are happening in our community and across the world, praying over Scripture, seeking to be sensitive to the leading of the Holy spirit – contributes to what I believe God wants me to share at Sunday services and at the midweek Bible study. For me, preaching is bringing the word of God relevantly to meet the needs of the congregation.
- preaching and teaching;
- regular pastoral visitation;
- administration;
- crisis counselling – dealing with whatever difficulties come up;
- providing overall leadership of and direction for the church;
- leadership in various committees in the church;
- church committees outside our own association of churches or even on a wider field, for example overseas teams;
- leadership training for leaders and potential leaders.

Deacon

Deacons manage the everyday running of the church. This means they look after practical affairs such as the care of the building and finances.

Team ministry

Baptist churches in general are increasingly moving towards the idea of team ministry, especially young churches. Magherafelt Baptist supports this idea. Their team is made up of three people: Clive (pastor), Jimmy (associate pastor) and Sharon (church worker). The team members report to each other and to the office-bearers (elders and deacons). Each member has responsibilities, some of which they share and others which are unique to their role. These are outlined below.

Teaching pastor

- teaching and preaching
- leadership
- pastoral care
- training

Associate pastor

- pastoral care
- evangelism
- support groups
- teaching and preaching

Church worker

- ministry coordinator
- administration coordinator
- mission team coordinator
- small group discipleship

Questions

1. **What qualities are required of an elder in the Baptist Church?**

2. **How do Baptist pastors dress for a Sunday service?**

3. **What is meant by the term 'team ministry'? How might team ministry improve the leadership of a Baptist church?**

 # KEY PERSONNEL IN THE CHURCH OF IRELAND

There are three main leadership positions in the Church of Ireland: **bishop**, **priest** and **deacon**.

Bishop

The term 'bishop' comes from the Greek word *episcopoi* which means 'overseer'. As such, the bishop is the leader of a local diocese. It is his job to 'guard the faith', to ordain and confirm. He has the ultimate responsibility of ensuring that the sacraments are properly administered in his diocese. Only the bishop can carry out the ordination of priests and deacons, and administer confirmation.

Priest

Every diocese is divided into parishes, each of which is usually cared for by a parish priest (often simply referred to as a **minister**).

The person in charge of a parish is usually a **rector**, often assisted by one or two **curates** (an assistant minister).

Training

Both men and women can be priests in the Church of Ireland, although all ministers must be **ordained**. This involves a period of training, involving the study of theology and time spent ministering in a church environment.

Dress

The standard everyday dress for a minister of the Church of Ireland usually includes a **clerical collar**, and when conducting a worship service they generally put on special garments such as a **cassock** (a long black robe), a **surplice** (a white overgarment) and a **scarf**.

Duties

The main duties of a Church of Ireland priest are to teach and preach the word of God and to administer the sacraments of baptism and communion to the people in their care. Canon Lloyd from Ballymena outlines some of the duties he carries out:

It is impossible to give an outline of a typical week, but here is a list of some of the tasks and jobs which I carry out:

– preparation for worship including sermon writing;

– daily prayer and meditation;

– stimulating and planning the ministry of the church;

– drawing out the ministry gifts of people;

– Christian nurture, for example encouraging and training Sunday School teachers and house group leaders;

– preparation for baptism;

– marriage preparation classes;

– funerals, pastoring the bereaved and visiting the sick;

– visitation of schools;

– school management (board of governors);

– parish administration, staff management and training;

– overseeing and assisting with youth and uniformed organisations;

– interviewing, training and managing adults who assist with children's work;

– chairing of committees;

– attending inter-church meetings and community meetings;

– dealing with conflict and maintaining unity within the church.

Deacon

The term deacon comes from the Greek word *diakonos* meaning 'helper'. Deacons in the Church of Ireland are usually trainee ministers who serve in a church for one year before their ordination.

A deacon helps the rector in taking the services. He or she carries out most of the normal duties of a rector or curate, assisting at Holy Communion and baptising children. A deacon also cares for the members of the parish by visiting the sick and elderly and being actively involved in youth work.

Member of the select vestry

The select vestry is a committee responsible for the finance, fabric and furnishings of a church, although it often has an important influence on other matters. As a result, the members of the select vestry are regarded as having a leadership role within the parish church. William is the secretary of a select vestry in a Co Antrim parish:

I have been a member of the select vestry for over 40 years and the secretary for nearly 30 years. As a secretary I am responsible for taking the minutes at the vestry meetings and dealing with all church correspondence which relates to the finances and maintenance of the church buildings. I also help to organise special events such as the yearly civic service when we invite people who represent all aspects of life in our town to a special church service. Another important role I play is as a 'sounding board' for the rector – he would often want to know my opinion about certain matters in order to understand the views of the congregation.

My job in the select vestry is very important to me and I get a great deal of satisfaction from it. I have a great love of my church and its liturgy and I find that carrying out my duties as a member of the select vestry is a way in which I can express my faith and beliefs – it is a form of service.

Lay reader

A lay reader holds an important position in the Church of Ireland. Readers are authorised to conduct services such as morning and evening prayer and to preach; however, they are not allowed to administer baptism or Holy Communion.

Worship leader

He or she is responsible for the music and singing.

Questions

1. What is the role of a bishop in the Church of Ireland?

2. How does the original Greek word for deacon help to explain the role of a deacon the Church of Ireland?

3. What is the select vestry and how might a member of the select vestry contribute to the life of the church?

KEY PERSONNEL IN THE METHODIST CHURCH

Minister

There are three main types of clergy in the Methodist church: **superintendents**, **ministers** and **voluntary ministers**.

Superintendents are responsible for groups of churches called circuits. Each of these individual churches is known as a **society**, which may or may not have a minister assigned to it. The voluntary ministers are ordained ministers who work voluntarily for the church, such as retired ministers, or those who are employed in another job and work part-time for the church.

Training

Methodist ministers are normally trained to university level, although there is a degree of flexibility in this. Their training lasts five years: usually three years in college and two years 'on circuit', working under the supervision of a superintendent minister.

In college their training includes studies in theology, the Old and New Testaments, church history and practical theology.

Dress

A Methodist minister normally wears a **clerical collar** during worship. Occasionally, at weddings or funerals, the minister wears a **cassock** which is a long outer robe. However, practices vary across Methodist churches.

Duties

The Reverend Heather Morris explains her job as a minister:

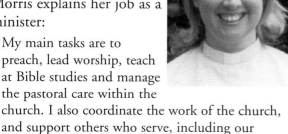

My main tasks are to preach, lead worship, teach at Bible studies and manage the pastoral care within the church. I also coordinate the work of the church, and support others who serve, including our voluntary minister and the church class leaders. A minister is also a community worker and is often involved in representing or working in the local community. It is difficult to define a typical week, as emergencies arise often and plans must be changed. However, in general the activities which make up the week are:
– preparation for sermons and Bible study;
– pastoral visiting those who are ill and going through particular difficulties as well as routine visiting;
– supporting and coordinating staff;
– prayer;
– evening meetings of action teams, and calling in to other church activities;
– vestry hour;
– related activities.

Local preacher

Local preachers are lay people who receive some training and are qualified to preach in Methodist churches, although they cannot baptise or lead a communion service. There are a large number of local preachers in the Methodist Church in Ireland and over half of all Sunday services are conducted by them. Although they are very involved in the life of their local church, the majority of local preachers have other careers as well. One such local preacher is Sheila:

As a local preacher, I feel I am following in a tradition begun by John Wesley, who sent out his preachers on horseback in all weathers. We still go out in all weathers, but in more comfort!

As an ordinary person with a job, I find preaching can be an exhausting and yet very fulfilling task. I don't have any other gifts which I can use in the church so, as this seems to be something which I can do, I feel I must. I feel my job is to address issues which affect people in their everyday lives, and to place these into the context of the Kingdom of Heaven.

Bringing a message to people on a Sunday is a heavy responsibility and I spend a lot of time on preparation. Through this, my own understanding is increased tremendously and this is very rewarding.

Society steward

The society stewards are the senior lay leaders. They support the minister in prayer and in decision making, and are responsible for some of the practical aspects of church life.

Class leaders

The congregation is divided into classes, each with a class leader. The class leader visits once a quarter, or as necessary, and if particular pastoral needs arise, will report back to the minister.

Specialist workers

It is common for Methodist churches to employ trained staff who are able to assist in specific aspects of the church's work, for example, family and community workers and youth workers.

Questions

1. **What are the main differences between a minister and a local preacher in the Methodist Church?**
2. **What do Methodist ministers normally wear when carrying out their duties?**
3. **Explain how the Methodist Church ensures that the pastoral needs of the congregation are met.**

KEY PERSONNEL IN THE PRESBYTERIAN CHURCH

Minister

There are three main types of minister in the Presbyterian Church: leading, assistant and associate. An **assistant** is someone who has just come out of college. The final stage of training is to work alongside an experienced minister, sharing the main duties. After a period as an assistant, the individual in question will then be fully ordained. An **associate** is someone who is already ordained but does not have a congregation of their own; instead, they have chosen to specialise in a particular type of ministry and would be called by a church for a limited period to do a specific job such as youth work or evangelism.

Training

All ministers in the Presbyterian Church must be trained to university level. It generally involves training for six years: three years to obtain a first degree and then three further years to do a theology degree, although those who are older can do a shorter course.

Dress

Traditionally Presbyterian ministers wear a **clerical collar**. When preaching this can be accompanied by a **robe**, like those worn at graduation ceremonies. Not many ministers wear the robe any longer and there are an increasing number who prefer more casual dress without a clerical collar.

Duties

The Reverend Graham Connor explains his main duties:

There are three key roles that I have in this church. Firstly, I teach the word of God, and that takes time for preparation and study. Traditionally ministers spend their morning doing that. Secondly, there is a pastoral role. Thirdly, I am a leader. A lot of my time is spent in leadership and working with other leaders: sowing a vision, building that vision and making it concrete. Often I initiate things, get people working with me and they end up doing them, a bit like the model Jesus presented with his disciples.

I would spend most mornings either doing study or administration, and increasingly there is more and more admin. I would also spend time during the day visiting hospitals or visiting the sick, dealing with bereavements, general visits, schools, and wider denominational things, for example lecturing in Union College. I work 60–70 hours in a week.

Elder

Every Presbyterian congregation has a board of **elders**, also called the **kirk session**. Usually there is approximately one elder appointed to look after the needs of 15–20 families in the church. The elders are responsible for visiting the families and giving communion tokens. Elders are considered to be different from the laity: while they are not clergy they have the same authority in the church as the minister.

The minister is considered to be the main teaching elder. In practice, the minister is seen as something slightly different from the others because he is full-time, but in the government of the church, the minister chairs the elders' meeting, with everyone having an equal say. The secretary of the kirk session (board of elders) is called the **clerk of session**. He is generally the key non-ministerial person in the church.

Elizabeth is a Presbyterian elder from Belfast:

As an elected elder I see my role as one of service to God and his church and as a frail human I am always open to advice and direction.
I am responsible for ten families within the congregation. I deliver communion tokens every second month and visit families at times of hardship and also to celebrate good news. I feel more confident approaching visits if I have prepared by prayer beforehand and of course discretion and

confidentiality are of the utmost importance. Within my particular church I try to give support to our minister by attending services regularly, helping to serve communion and occasionally reading the Bible lesson. I try to attend as many congregational functions as possible and although involvement may appear to be the duty of an elder I must confess that I see it as a pleasure to be part of the family in our church community.

Being an elder has provided me with an opportunity to reaffirm my beliefs and witness for Christ. Beyond the practical duties as an elder I feel I have developed in my spiritual life and I am also learning the true value and importance of relationships. I know that I sometimes fall short in loving my neighbour but I am encouraged by the realisation that God is here to help me with my aim in life. This is to mature a little more each day along the path of Christianity.

Deaconess

A deaconess does most of the work that a minister does, except preaching and giving the sacraments. She would do visiting, organisational work, pastoring and hospital work. There is no equivalent male role.

Worship director

The worship director is in charge of the choir, chooses music for performance in the Sunday service, and in consultation with the minister helps to coordinate the style of worship in the church.

Questions

1. **What is the difference between an assistant and an associate minister in the Presbyterian Church?**

2. **What is the traditional dress of a Presbyterian minister and how is this changing?**

3. **Outline the main duties of:**

   (a) an elder;

   (b) a deaconess.

✝ KEY PERSONNEL IN THE ROMAN CATHOLIC CHURCH

There are a large number of special roles and positions within the Catholic Church. The most senior roles include the **Pope**, **cardinals** and **archbishops**.

At a local level the people who are responsible for the leading and caring for individual members of the church are **bishops** and **priests**. Priests are assisted in their duties by others including **deacons**, **Eucharistic ministers** and **readers**.

The Pope

The Pope is the head of the Catholic Church and regarded as being Christ's representative on Earth. Catholics believe that during his lifetime Jesus gave his disciple Peter the authority to care for and lead his followers when he ascended to heaven (Matthew 18:18–19). This role is believed to have been passed on since Peter's time to successive Popes up to the present day.

Cardinal

Cardinals are an international team of the Pope's close advisors who have the responsibility of assisting the Pope and of electing a new Pope when required.

Archbishop and bishop

The Catholic Church is an **episcopal** church which means that the key leaders are the bishops. The word bishop comes from a Greek word meaning overseer and a bishop has responsibility for overseeing the church in his particular area (known as a diocese).

Some of the bishop's main responsibilities are:

– to ordain priests;

– to baptise and confirm new church members;

– to settle disputes in the church.

Priest

A parish priest is responsible for leading the worship in his church. He might be helped in this by an assistant priest, often called a **curate**.

Training

To become a priest a single man must complete a course of study (of at least six years' duration) at a seminary. Here he will study a range of subjects such as theology and philosophy, as well as carrying out a placement in his final year of seminary, for example in a children's home, hospice, youth centre, school, hospital or prison.

Dress

The traditional day-to-day dress of a parish priest is a black suit and a clerical collar. During worship a priest normally wears additional garments, such as an **alb**, a **cassock** and a **stole**.

Duties

Father Ciaran Dallat explains some of the key tasks a priest carries out:

One Vatican document emphasises that the role of the priest is to speak the word of God and then to administer the sacraments of baptism and the Eucharist, promote reconciliation and anoint the sick.

Other duties include visiting those in hospital, caring for the dying, working with schools as chaplains and sitting on their boards of governors. The priest also performs a role as a counsellor, for example in the case of marriage problems. The priest is a community leader and there is an expectation that he represents the people in his parish.

Deacon

In Ireland, deacons are men who have trained for the priesthood, but are awaiting their first full-time post.

In other countries there are deacons who are laypeople who work full-time or part-time in the church, assisting the priest with his duties.

Eucharistic minister

A Eucharistic minister is someone who assists in the distribution of the Eucharist (the bread) to the congregation during Mass. The role also involves bringing the Eucharist to those people who are unable to attend the service, perhaps because of illness.

John, a Eucharistic minister from south Belfast, explains what he gains from his role:

> At the lowest level it's a very practical form of helping out. On a personal level it's a privilege, a constant reminder of my own faith and my own duties and responsibilities in relation to that faith – it's a privilege to serve others.
>
> I myself have been a Eucharistic minister for 15 years and I find it a very rewarding experience to bring the sacrament to someone who is ill, whether in hospital or at home. I don't have as much time to do this as I used to but some people in our parish, usually retired people, spend an enormous amount of time doing this sort of work.
>
> I think participation of lay people enhances the whole worship experience for everyone, and I think that's a very important manifestation of the living faith.

Readers

Members of the Catholic Church are often asked to deliver the first or second reading in the Mass (only a priest or deacon can read the gospel). Members may also take part in reading the 'Prayers of the Faithful'.

Questions

1. **What are the main duties of:**

   (a) a bishop in the Catholic Church?

   (b) a priest in the Catholic Church?

2. **What does a priest normally wear during worship?**

3. **Explain how a Eucharistic minister might contribute to the life of the church.**

END OF UNIT REVIEW

End of Unit Questions

1. The word 'personnel' refers to the people who either work for a church or carry out particular jobs within a church on a voluntary basis. Choose two denominations you have studied and in your notebook copy and complete the table below.

Denomination	Key personnel	Main duties

2. "The main task of a church leader is to preach." Do you agree or disagree with this statement? Give reasons for your answer.

3. Ministers/pastors/priests are involved in many activities other than preaching. Select any two from the list below and explain why each one is important:

   – visiting the sick and bereaved;
   – preparing young people for confirmation;
   – preparing couples for marriage;
   – celebrating communion/Eucharist;
   – leading school assemblies;
   – private prayer and study;
   – encouraging church members in their roles and responsibilities in the church.

4. Why do some church leaders choose to wear special clothes? Do you agree or disagree with this idea? Give reasons for your opinion.

5. Look back at two of the churches you have studied in this unit and find out why people who are not ministers, priests or pastors take on leadership roles in local churches. How important do you think it is that churches involve members of the congregation in church leadership?

Activity

In pairs, discuss what type of person you think might make a good leader in a church. On paper, sketch a possible layout for a job advertisement for a minister in a particular denomination. The ad should include the title of the post; the church; a brief job description; essential qualifications/criteria; desirable qualifications/criteria; a deadline; and address for applications.

Once you have planned your layout and discussed what will be included in the advert, you can now produce your final copy. If you have access to a computer, you could use word processing or publishing software.

Activity

A Day in the Life of...

Using the information about the duties of a minister from one of the sections you have studied in this unit, try to imagine what a possible day in the life of a priest or minister would be like and prepare a desktop diary.

If you can interview or talk with a minister you know it would be even better.

You should also include notes in a 'tasks' section on what needs to be done in the next few days.

Learning outcomes

As a result of studying of this unit you should

- *understand the variety in the titles and roles of Christian leadership;*
- *examine the function of key personnel in two traditions;*
- *explore significant issues of difference in Christian thinking about the ordination of women, clerical dress and the theological importance of a priest or minister.*

Tips for exam success

A long answer question is testing more than just knowledge, so what are the examiners looking for in your answer? They want to see that you:

- *understand the question;*
- *have a sound knowledge of the topic or issue;*
- *can understand that there may be more than one way of looking at a controversial issue;*
- *can argue a point of view;*
- *can use relevant evidence to argue your point of view.*

Church organisation and government 6

INTRODUCTION

'Church government' is a rather grand title which simply means how churches are organised and what kind of leadership they have. Some denominations are very highly organised like a large company in which each individual church is a small part. Also, like a large company or a state government, it has many layers of authority, with the most important person at the top. Others like to keep a more flexible and less structured style, even to the point of having no one person in charge of a church.

There are many arguments for and against these styles of church government. It would not be possible for us to study all the types of church government that exist in churches in Ireland so we will concentrate on three main styles, but it is important to note that some churches may use one or more of the types described below.

1. The episcopal model

An episcopal church is one that is governed by bishops. It is also considered to be a **hierarchical** form of church government which means that there is a clear line of command in the organisation, from archbishop to bishop to priest to deacon.

A central part of the organisation of episcopal churches is the **diocese**. This is the area a bishop is in charge of. A diocese is simply a collection of local or parish churches from a particular region of a country. For example, Down and Dromore is a diocese of the Church of Ireland and includes churches in parts of County Antrim, County Down and Belfast.

The episcopal model of church government was one type of government that emerged during the first 300 years of the church for two main reasons.

- **To prevent false teaching and maintain unity** – a common problem in the first years of the church occurred when Christians had different opinions about their faith. Some of these ideas were so different to what the majority of Christians believed that they were considered to be dangerous distortions of the truth. It was important therefore to have a strong leader in each church who taught the 'right beliefs'. If a group of leaders were able to agree, then it was possible to develop a sense of unity and agreement between churches.

- **To create a strong organisation** – during the first 300 years of the Christian Church the Christians were often persecuted by the Roman Empire. They could easily have been destroyed if they had become disorganised and had fallen out with each other. It was important to have strong leaders who could make decisions in a crisis and be an example to others.

Many Christians believe that it is still important today to have a form of government which brings unity and strength and which sets out clearly the beliefs of the church.

2. The representative model

The representative form of church government is, like the episcopal model, highly structured. In this case, however, there are no bishops.

It can be called a representative form of government because decisions are made at councils made up of ministers and clergy who represent the opinions of their congregations. This can be compared to how Members of Parliament represent their constituencies in the House of Commons. In this case, the process of government is two-way because leaders have the authority to make decisions only if the people whom they represent are happy with them.

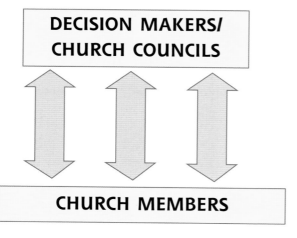

The representative form of church government first appeared during the Protestant Reformation of the sixteenth century for several reasons, including the following.

- **To prevent corruption in the church** – during the Reformation one of the main complaints of the reformers was that many leaders in the Catholic Church were abusing their authority and not living in a moral way.

  One way to make sure this would not happen in their newly formed churches, some Protestants felt, was to establish a representative form of government.

- **To give individuals more responsibility** – the Reformation occurred at a time when people were challenging authority in many ways and taking more responsibility for their own decisions.

  This was also the goal for the reformers in matters of faith and religion.

3. The autonomous/ congregational model

This model places power in the hands of each church member. There is no hierarchy; each church is regarded as equal and capable of making its own decisions, although in reality there are some very general rules which all churches do abide by.

Autonomous means self-governing, but the organisational structure of this model might best be described as a **network** in which churches with shared beliefs have contact with each other but no authority over each other. There is no central body that makes decisions which affect all the churches.

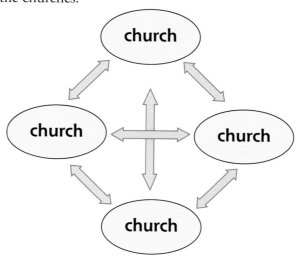

The autonomous model also came about as a result of the Protestant Reformation, but became popular in its present form during the eighteenth and nineteenth centuries for several reasons, including the following.

- **To stress the 'priesthood of all believers'** – this is the idea that all Christians are equal before God and should therefore not be obedient to any rules or human institutions, including church governments, but only to God directly. They can discover what God expects of them from reading the Bible.

- **To reflect the worship of the early Church as described in the Bible** – those who support this model of church government argue that there is no mention of any organised church government in the Bible. Indeed, in the book of Acts the Christians seem to gather in a community in which everyone has equal rights. Paul's letters are also cited as evidence of each Christian group making their own decisions and managing their own affairs.

Activity

As these models show, there are some important issues or questions when it comes to church government. Here are just a few for you to think about:

1. *How important is it to have strong leadership and clear rules in a church?*

2. *What are the benefits of the autonomous model?*

3. *How important is it that churches within a denomination are united in their teachings and beliefs?*

4. *If Christians believe that God is in control, why is it important that individual members of a church should have their views represented at a meeting of the church government?*

BAPTIST CHURCH GOVERNMENT

The Baptist Church in Ireland is typical of the autonomous/congregational model of church government. Each church regards itself as **independent** and there is no formal structure of church government. However, Baptist churches are also **inter-dependent** in that they frequently work together in order to share resources or to provide assistance to other churches, and this requires some coordination.

The Association of Baptist Churches in Ireland

The Association of Baptist Churches in Ireland is the name given to the fellowship of Baptist churches that work together. It has a permanent office with a variety of departments and officers

dealing with a range of activities including missionary work, youth work, education and welfare. The work of the Association is overseen by a **Church Council**. Every church sends a representative twice a year to a council where decisions are made. Such decisions may affect local churches (for example, there is a 'Statement of Faith' that all churches which belong to the Association must adhere to) while others may be purely organisational or administrative matters.

If a special issue arises, the Association would meet to vote, but on the whole its purpose is to support, encourage and strengthen the work of individual churches.

While the Association of Baptist Churches in Ireland cannot interfere in the beliefs and worship of individual churches, a church may withdraw from the Association if it feels that it cannot agree with the other members of the Association. As a result there are a small number of independent Baptist churches in Ireland.

Local level

At a local level decisions are made in two ways. For routine matters concerning the spiritual life of the church, a group of **elders** would provide leadership and be involved in pastoral duties.

However, on more significant issues a decision must be made by the members of the local church. Before a decision is reached people are given two weeks' notice for a members' meeting. If it is expected to be a short meeting, it might be held after a Sunday morning service.

However, for very important decisions the members would arrange a special meeting at which two-thirds of the church membership would have to be present for a vote to be valid.

Questions

1. *Give some examples of the work carried out by the Association of Baptist Churches in Ireland.*

2. *Explain how important decisions are made in local Baptist churches in Ireland.*

CHURCH OF IRELAND GOVERNMENT

The style of government in the Church of Ireland could be said to be both **episcopal** *and* **representative**. In many ways the organisation of the Church of Ireland reflects traditional forms of government in the UK. No one person has absolute control. Rather, there is a parliament called a **synod**, made up of representatives who have been elected by the local churches to make decisions. However, the synod, unlike parliament, only meets once a year and there are other bodies who carry on the work of the synod from one year to the next. This is also the case at diocesan level. The diagram below illustrates the different tiers of government.

Area of responsibility	Decision-making body	Day-to-day administration	Chair/person responsible
National Church	General synod	Standing committee	Archbishop
Diocese	Diocesan synod	Diocesan committee	Bishop
Parish	Select vestry	Parish clergy	Rector/minister

Decision-making bodies

Select vestry

Each parish church or a group of churches within a parish will have a select vestry. These are members of the church who help the clergy run the church. Technically they have responsibility for finance and fabric and furnishings, but in reality in most parishes they also have a wider leadership role. Any member of the congregation who submits their name to an electoral register is entitled to vote when the members of the select vestry are elected yearly. The leading minister of the parish will usually be the chairperson of the select vestry.

Diocesan synod

Once a year, representatives from each parish within a diocese meet to hold a synod. The council is made up of clergy and lay people from each church and is chaired by the bishop. The diocesan synod is a channel through which the business of the church flows in two directions. It has the responsibility and power to implement decisions that have been taken at the General Synod, but also has the authority to make resolutions and statements about matters of concern to the diocese and to take these forward for consideration at national level when the General Synod meets.

General Synod

Although the Church of Ireland has an episcopalian form of government, its members would argue that it is also representative and democratic – that is, all members of the church are represented through those who attend the synods. The General Synod is made up of three main groups: bishops, clergy and laity. Each member's vote has equal weight.

The General Synod has the power to put forward resolutions, discuss bills and pass **statutes**. A law of the church begins life as a resolution, which is a type of proposal. In order to become a part of church law, a resolution must then be discussed as a bill and passed three times by the General Synod. At this point it becomes a statute and part of the law of the church.

International organisation

The Church of Ireland has links with other national Anglican churches around the world, including the Church of England, the Episcopal Church of Scotland and the Episcopalian Church in America. Although historically all Anglican churches grew out of the Church of England, it has no authority over any other national church.

International links can also be developed at parish and diocesan level when churches share joint ventures or become twinned with churches in other countries.

Questions

1. Explain how the views and opinions of Church of Ireland members are represented at different levels of church government.

2. How is the Church of Ireland connected to other churches around the world?

METHODIST CHURCH GOVERNMENT

The style of government in the Methodist Church in Ireland is most like the **representative** model of church government. Methodists, however, use another word to describe their particular form of representative government – **connexional**. This suggests that the leaders of the Methodist Church do not rule over the individual churches but are connected with them in a strong link which is a two-way process.

The highest decision-making body in the Methodist Church is the **Conference**.

Area of responsibility	Decision-making body	Chair/person responsible
Methodist Church in Ireland	Conference	President
District	District synod	District superintendent
Circuit	Quarterly board	Superintendent minister
Local society	Leaders' meeting	Minister

Decision-making bodies

Methodist Conference

Conference is the main legislative and decision-making body in the Methodist Church in Ireland. It is made up of an equal number of ministers and lay representatives, each with equal voting rights. There is a **president** who is elected by the Conference and who serves for one year.

District synod

Within the Methodist Church, Ireland is divided into eight districts, each of which is headed by a **district superintendent** who chairs a district synod made up of ministers and leaders from the churches in that district. The district synod can raise issues to be discussed at conference level as well as having general responsibility for issues such as the management of buildings and the development of the work and worship of the church within the district. The district superintendent is elected by the synod and serves for three years.

Quarterly board

Within each district are circuits that are headed by a **superintendent minister**. Each circuit usually has a number of churches that may or may not have a minister assigned to each one. Decisions made by local societies at a leaders' meeting must usually be agreed at a quarterly board meeting.

Leaders' meeting

Each individual church is known as a **society** (one minister may serve a number of societies). Decisions concerning individual societies are made at a leaders' meeting which is attended by the local minister and church leaders.

International organisation

Internationally the Methodist Church in Ireland has links with other national Methodist churches around the world. Because of its proximity and historical links, it has a particularly strong relationship with the British Methodist Church.

One of the ways in which international links are formed is through sending and receiving mission partners.

Questions

1. The style of government in the Methodist Church is described as being 'connexional'. What does this mean?

2. What function does a district synod play in the government of the Methodist Church in Ireland?

PRESBYTERIAN CHURCH GOVERNMENT

The Presbyterian Church in Ireland could be described as being a **representative** form of church government. It is made up of four main decision-making bodies called the **court** of the church. Each court has a **moderator** who chairs the meeting, and a secretary called a **clerk**.

Area of responsibility	Decision-making body	Day-to-day administration	Chair/person responsible
Presbyterian Church in Ireland	General Assembly	Boards of the General Assembly	General Moderator
Regional area	Synod	N/A	Moderator
District	Presbytery	N/A	Moderator
Congregation	Kirk session	Minister	Minister

Decision-making bodies

General Assembly

The General Assembly is the **supreme court** of the Presbyterian Church in Ireland and makes major decisions for the church. Every minister is able to attend the General Assembly and each congregation sends one minister and one elder, who have equal voting rights. A different **Moderator** of the Assembly is elected every year.

The Boards of the General Assembly tend to deal with issues of a practical rather than a theological nature. For example there are boards for youth, education and overseas mission.

Synod

There are five synods in Ireland and each congregation sends one minister and one elder to their regional synod. These normally meet once a year, although in recent years many of the functions of the synod have been subsumed in the work of the presbyteries.

Presbytery

Presbyteries are generally made up of about 24 churches and meet about seven or eight times a year. There are 21 district presbyteries in Ireland.

Like the synod and the General Assembly, each church within a presbytery is represented at a presbytery meeting by a minister and one elder.

The presbytery deals with local business and business sent down from the Assembly, and would occasionally make visits to individual churches.

Kirk session

The kirk session is a committee which has the responsibility for making decisions at an individual congregational level. It is made up of elected elders and the minister.

International organisation

The Presbyterian Church in Ireland has links at international level through the **World Alliance of Reformed Churches**.

They also have historical links with other Presbyterian churches, for instance the Church of Scotland, denominations in America and some in Africa and eastern Europe.

Questions

1. What are the main responsibilities of the General Assembly in the Presbyterian Church?

2. What is the difference between a presbytery and a kirk session?

ROMAN CATHOLIC CHURCH GOVERNMENT

The Catholic Church is a clear example of a **hierarchical** and **episcopal** style of church government. In practice this means that the church is governed primarily by **bishops** who are directly responsible to the Pope in Rome.

The bishops connect the local churches in their diocese with the international Catholic Church.

Area of responsibility	Decision-making body	Day-to-day administration	Chair/person responsible
Worldwide RC Church	College of Bishops	Curia	Pope
The Catholic Church in Ireland	Irish Catholic Bishops' Conference	Various Commissions	Archbishop of Armagh or Cardinal
Diocese	N/A	Diocesan office	Bishop
Parish	Pastoral councils	Parish clergy	Priest

Decision-making bodies

College of bishops

This is the highest decision-making body in the Catholic Church. However, there are thousands of bishops in the Catholic Church and so it is very rare for a meeting to be held when all the bishops would be present – in fact, in the last two centuries it has happened only twice! These meetings were called **Vatican I** and **Vatican II** and each took place over several years. Whatever decisions are reached at such meetings are binding on the whole Catholic Church.

Episcopal conference

This is a meeting of bishops at a national or regional level which takes place about once a year. Bishops from Northern Ireland and the Republic of Ireland attend an episcopal conference which is called the **Irish Catholic Bishops' Conference**. This is an opportunity for bishops to discuss important issues and to formulate statements which express their opinion on contemporary issues. However, the conference does not actually have any power to make rules or to instruct bishops how to act.

Bishop

On a day-to-day basis the most important decision-making authority in the Catholic Church is not a committee or a council but a person, the bishop, who is responsible for a group of parish churches called a **diocese**. The diocese of Down and Connor covers all of County Antrim, Belfast and part of County Down, comprising 88 parishes. There are 26 dioceses in Ireland which are grouped into four **archdiocese** – Armagh, Dublin, Cashel and Tuam – each under an archbishop. Each bishop has total control of what goes on in his diocese and is answerable only to the Pope or a college of bishops.

Priest/pastoral council

At the parish level all decisions are traditionally taken by the local priests. However, in recent years there has been an attempt to involve more of the congregation in the life and work of the church.

Many parishes now have pastoral councils which help to direct and lead the spiritual life and activity of a local church.

Questions

1. What is a diocese?
2. Outline the role of the episcopal conference in Ireland.
3. How might pastoral councils improve church government at a local level in the Catholic Church?

END OF UNIT REVIEW

1. *Name three main styles of church government.*

2. *What are the advantages and disadvantages of an autonomous form of church government?*

3. *Choose any Christian denomination and describe how it is organised. You might want to copy the 'writing frame' below into your book to help you, or design your own writing frame, using word-processing software.*

Style of church government	Main forms of government at a local level
Main forms of government at national and international level	How important decisions are made in the church

4. *"It is important that church governments are organised in a hierarchy so everyone knows who is in charge and what they believe." Discuss this statement, showing that you have considered more than one point of view.*

Activity

You and several others have been asked to take charge of the running of your local church youth club.

1. *In a group, decide how you would organise the club and the 'system of government' you would use. As part of your discussion you need to consider:*

   - *how you will make decisions;*

   - *what responsibilities each member of the group will have;*

   - *how to deal with bad behaviour at the youth club;*

   - *how to deal with complaints;*

   - *how you will make sure your money is spent properly;*

   - *what relationships you will establish with other organisations within the church and who you consider to be your 'boss';*

   - *what control you will give to other individuals or committees.*

2. *Once you have discussed these things, you must then design an 'About Us' web page for your group which might appear on the youth club website. This will describe how the youth club is run and who is in charge and the rules which anyone attending must obey.*

3. *Now review the kind of club you have organised.*

   - *Would you describe it as being hierarchical or representative in its style of government?*

   - *Why do you think your style of government will work best?*

   - *Present your web page to the rest of the class and explain why you have organised the youth club in the way that you have.*

4. *Using your experiences, look again at the questions in the Activity on page 111.*

Have your opinions changed at all?

Tips for exam success

Questions which include a phrase like 'consider more than one point of view in your answer' require you to structure your answer in the style of a discussion.

It is helpful if you can make it clear who holds the opinions you are expressing. Otherwise you should use language like 'some Christians believe that . . . while others think . . .'

Of course you can build an argument, supported by evidence, which is in line with your own point of view.

The important thing is that you can give examples of arguments used by others who would disagree with you.

Learning outcomes

The study of this unit will allow the reader to

– understand three different models of church government and some reasons behind the development of each;

– examine the style of church government in two traditions.

Interdenominational contacts

ECUMENISM AND THE WORLD COUNCIL OF CHURCHES

The divisions, wars and conflicts which have been caused by differences among Christians are well known, but before, during and after the Reformation there have also been Christians who have felt strongly that, whatever the differences in religious outlook, Christians from every denomination should be able to get along with one another.

During the 20th century many churches in Europe began to realise that they could work more effectively if they joined forces, particularly in missionary work and when helping those in need. Eventually, many denominations around the world agreed to cooperate on these issues, and acknowledged the benefits of greater unity among Christians by forming the **World Council of Churches** in **1948**. Churches who are committed to working together in this way are often referred to as **ecumenical**. The word ecumenism comes from a Greek word, *oikumene*, which means 'worldwide' or 'the whole inhabited world'.

Find out more about WCC from their website at www.wcc-coe.org/wcc/english.html

The World Council of Churches has two main aims:

1. Unity – the World Council of Churches believes that The Christian Church should be global and united to try to fulfil Jesus' prayer for believers, "that all of them may be one" (John 17:20-22). It encourages churches to discuss their theological differences and find ways of resolving them.

2. To help people in need – the World Council of Churches has its headquarters in **Geneva**, Switzerland, and is very involved in an ongoing programme of aid and relief work, as well as a determined effort to influence governments to act in a fair and just way.

Activity

What is the Biblical basis for unity?

Look up the following references and explain how a Christian might use each to argue for the importance of interdenominational contacts:
- *Luke 10:25–28*
- *John 17:22–23*
- *1 Corinthians 12:12–31*
- *Ephesians 4:4–5*

Attitudes to ecumenism

There are mixed feelings in local churches about ecumenism. Some denominations feel strongly opposed to the idea and prefer not to get involved in any activities which might be called **ecumenical**. There are a variety of reasons for this. For example, they believe that in order to reach agreement with Christians from other traditions they would have to compromise their personal beliefs, and they might argue that they cannot consider their church to be equal to another church which has 'wrong' beliefs.

On the other hand there are those who are keen supporters of ecumenism and are proud to be members of the World Council of Churches. One supporter of ecumenism from the Church of Ireland, Ian Ellis, says that ecumenism is "the search for agreement in faith and order and for unity in the Churches' life . . . It is about being Christians together" (*A Tapestry of Beliefs*).

Finally, there are those who would not call themselves 'ecumenical' but would be happy to participate in some inter-church activity in their local area. For this reason the terms **interdenominational** or **inter-church** are now more commonly used to describe the work and activities of Christians from different backgrounds who are committed to the importance of maintaining good relationships and working together on issues of mutual concern.

Activity

Opinions on Ecumenism from Churches in NI

Look at these comments on inter-church contacts from the churches we have visited and discuss the questions over the page. Keep in mind that they represent the outlook of their own local congregation, but not necessarily the whole denomination. Other churches from similar denominations may be more or less involved in this work.

Baptist

We don't have formal links with other churches but lots of informal links – that is something we would like to cultivate. True Biblical ecumenism means a union of heart and spirit among believers rather than trying to bring together structures or denominations. This is reflected in a statement from the Baptist churches' Council in 1997: "Recognising the diversity that exists in the Body of Christ, we re-affirm our desire to foster spiritual unity with all those who love the Lord Jesus Christ in sincerity and who are faithful to His gospel."

In our local church we have dialogue with the local Roman Catholic church. I believe that if I am a genuine Christian then my friendship should be to all.

Pastor Clive Johnston

Church of Ireland

There is a Ballymena inter-church group for clergy, which I participate in, and one for lay people. In this parish there are only a few people who would be actively committed to inter-church relationships and attend the inter-church group. They organise joint activities, seminars and visits and sometimes they worship together.

Canon Stuart Lloyd

Methodist

There is a deep commitment to supporting and working alongside other Christian churches in our area. The minister meets frequently with the ministers of churches in our local area to pray together. There are shared services with local Anglican and Presbyterian churches quarterly and every Sunday evening in the summer. We also work together on joint projects such as a Summer Scheme for young people.

Reverend Heather Morris

Presbyterian

In this area the ministers meet regularly – the Church of Ireland, Methodist, Congregational, the City Mission and ourselves. We meet to pray together and are planning a joint service next Easter.

The local Catholic church is linked with other Protestant churches up the road. We have had some small links with them and we encourage that. This congregation would not, however, be keen on ecumenism and we as a denomination removed ourselves from the WCC some years ago. Ecumenism in the Presbyterian Church in Ireland happens on a local level – some churches are very involved and some aren't.

Reverend Graham Connor

Roman Catholic

I believe that Jesus is present in every Christian equally and we should be working more together. In particular I feel that young people from different denominations should be encouraged to have contacts with each other. In my role as university chaplain I regularly work alongside clergy from Protestant churches to plan activities and events for students from different Christian backgrounds, and we share one space for worship on the university campus.

Unfortunately, we have no ecumenical links in our parish, although I personally would like to see some established.

Father Ciaran Dallat

INTER-CHURCH CONTACTS IN NORTHERN IRELAND

Those involved in inter-church contacts do not try to pretend that differences in belief and practice do not exist. There are certain things in every denomination that are unique and valued by its members.

However, those committed to inter-church work believe that it is possible for Christians to come together in a united way and also in a way which allows those from different denominations to value and maintain their own traditions and beliefs.

Inter-church contacts can take place on three levels:

1. National level
2. Local clerical level
3. Local lay level

National level

At a national level there are two main organisations on the island of Ireland – **The Irish Council of Churches** and the **Irish Inter-Church Meeting**. The Irish Council of Churches was formed in **1923** to help Protestant churches come closer together and work more effectively in areas of social concern.

During the 1970s it was felt important that there should be greater communication between Catholic and Protestant traditions on issues of common concern, such as violence in Northern Ireland. The result was the setting up of the Irish Inter-Church Meeting comprising the members of the Irish Council of Churches along with the Catholic Church. The Irish Inter-Church Meeting continues to meet regularly and discuss issues of a social and theological nature.

Local clerical and local lay levels

It is common for groups of local ministers to meet together to discuss issues of common concern, to keep each other informed about events being planned and, on some occasions, to agree to work together.

The most common way that church members from different denominations meet is through shared activities; for example, running joint parent and toddler groups, inviting one another to charity events or sharing resources for a youth club. In some cases churches will worship together and organise special ecumenical services (see case study 1).

There are also certain organisations in Northern Ireland which provide opportunities for ordinary people from different backgrounds and traditions to meet together and learn about each other. These are referred to as **reconciliation projects**. Perhaps the most famous is the **Corrymeela** community based in Ballycastle, Co Antrim.

The Corrymeela community

The Corrymeela community was established in **1965** by the **Rev Ray Davey** who was the Presbyterian chaplain at Queen's University, Belfast. The purpose of the centre is to encourage reconciliation among people in Ireland, both north and south, and throughout the world. There are 200 members of the Corrymeela community who belong to different denominations and are committed to breaking down the barriers that exist between Protestant and Catholic people in our community. The community believes that barriers can be broken down by:

- providing a safe space where people feel valued and accepted;
- providing opportunity for dialogue in communities to dispel ignorance and prejudice and encourage mutual respect and cooperation;
- supporting local activists in community interface areas to find alternatives to violence;
- supporting victims of violence and injustice;
- enabling the healing of personal and social wounds;
- promoting new initiatives for social and political change;
- addressing contemporary issues of faith and ethics;
- developing new expressions of Christian faith and worship.

One important part of its work is the running of residential programmes for youth, school, community, family and church groups.

A gathering for worship at Corrymeela.

Activity

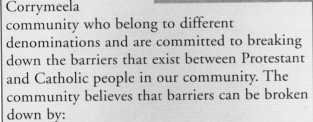

There are a number of other local reconciliation projects; information about some of them is given below. Try to find some further details about one project. Think carefully about how to present your findings to the rest of your class. You might try to use some form of ICT, if it is available, to design a leaflet using a desktop publishing package such as Microsoft Publisher or create a PowerPoint presentation to present to the whole class. The following headings may give you some ideas to help you organise your information: 'Origins/Background to the project', 'Aims of the project', 'Examples of work or activities carried out by the project', 'Your opinion about the value of the project'.

Reconciliation Projects:

The Cornerstone Community, 445 Springfield Road, Belfast, BT12 7DL

YouthLink www.youthlink.org.uk

The Christian Renewal Centre, http://www.crc-rostrevor.org/

The Glencree Centre for Reconciliation http://www.glencree-cfr.ie/

Case study 1 – Fitzroy Presbyterian Church

The Reverend Ken Newell is a minister in Fitzroy Presbyterian Church in south Belfast. His church is actively involved in inter-church contacts with **Clonard Monastery**, a Roman Catholic church in west Belfast.

Ken describes himself as having grown up with an anti-Catholic mindset shaped by his local community. He was fundamentalist in outlook, with a closed mind and a negative attitude towards the Roman Catholic Church. He had no close Roman Catholic friends before the age of 18.

After training as a Presbyterian minister, Ken went as a missionary to Indonesia. Here he felt that God broadened his horizons and he recognised that Christ's family included the Roman Catholic Church.

Ken returned to Belfast and in 1976 took up his present post in Fitzroy where he has worked hard to overcome the religious divisions in Northern Ireland.

1. Can you describe some of the practical ways in which your congregation makes contact with others?

• Prayer and Bible study

Every month the 'Fitzroy–Clonard Group' meets. This is an inter-church fellowship which was founded in 1981 and is made up of members of Fitzroy Presbyterian Church in south Belfast and Clonard Monastery in west Belfast. They meet to study the Bible and listen to talks given by prominent Presbyterian and Catholic scholars and theologians.

• Worship

We have joint services where there is singing, scripture reading, preaching and prayer. Periodically, the Clonard choir combines with our own choir to lead worship in our respective churches.

Concerning the Lord's Supper, which is celebrated each month in Fitzroy, all who love Christ are invited to participate and this includes our Catholic Christian friends, if they wish.

There is not yet within the Catholic Church the same freedom for other Christians to receive communion. We respect each other's church traditions and leaders. But we also vigorously discuss the issues involved.

• Working together in mission

The mission we are involved in is a peace mission. From 1990 to 1993 private talks were initiated in Clonard between a small group of Protestant and Catholic clergy and lay members and leaders from Sinn Féin. A similar and parallel dialogue continued in Fitzroy and in other venues with loyalist paramilitary groupings. Our goal was to help terminate the violence and to promote a democratic resolution of the conflict.

It seemed an impossible task at the beginning. But several months after the talks ended, ceasefires were announced.

• Serving the community

We reach out to the community in different ways. Following the 11 September disaster in the United States, we organised a public meeting in Fitzroy entitled 'Dying for your Faith'. We invited leaders of the Muslim and Jewish communities to join Presbyterian and Catholic speakers. The place was packed.

We also serve the community through our ongoing work for peace and reconciliation.

• Developing a sense of fellowship

Fellowship is really about friendship. And for friendships to develop you need to give people time. Today the friendships between the members of Fitzroy and Clonard are relaxed and strong. We develop opportunities to deepen them.

Last summer 30 of us went to Donegal together for five days. We visited ancient Celtic sites as well as local Presbyterian and Catholic congregations. The welcome we received was warm and generous. The local church members shared with us the history of their faith communities.

2. How does the Bible support your views?

In the Genesis creation story we read that God created Adam and Eve to be friends and partners. Conflict in the family led to them becoming hostile towards each other. Cain and Abel, their children, started to fight and damage each other.

This ancient story mirrors our world today. It is full of conflict, whether at an international level, at local level, and frequently in families. People find it hard to get on with one another. They undermine more than they support each other and build walls to separate themselves. Belfast has dozens of them.

Christ came to break down those barriers. He himself was very free in his friendships. He befriended not only those of his own religion, the Jews, but went to the people that everybody else looked down upon – hostile political opponents, 'unsound' Samaritans, and 'alien' Gentiles.

In his ministry, Jesus befriended everybody. In his death he embraced the whole world. In his resurrection he created a church that is inclusive – both men and women, slave and free, rich and poor, Jew and Gentile, black and white, Protestant and Catholic, nationalist and unionist.

God's church should be inclusive, affirming and ready to build bridges between people. It should be a place where there is no sexism, racism, ageism or sectarianism.

3. In your opinion, what would need to change in Northern Ireland for interdenominational contacts to improve?

I believe it is the responsibility of the clergy, as the leaders of the church, to open their hearts to the other side and give the hand of friendship.

This makes it easier for their congregations to follow their lead.

Change the clergy and you change the members. Change the members and you change the country.

Questions

1. *"If Christianity is to survive in the twenty-first century, the denominations need to focus on what they have in common rather than on their differences."*

   Do you agree or disagree with this statement?

2. *Explain why Christians of different denominations might choose to worship together.*

Case study 2 – Lisburn Inter-Church Group

The Lisburn Inter-Church project was set up in 1996 as a practical way for churches in Lisburn to work together. Kerry Nicholson, the full-time worker with the project, sets the scene:

The churches involved are First Lisburn Presbyterian, Railway Street Presbyterian, St Columba's Presbyterian, the Methodist Church, Harmony Hill Presbyterian, Lisburn Church of Ireland Cathedral, Seymour Street Methodist, St Patrick's Catholic and St Colman's Catholic.

We have premises in Lisburn town centre which is a neutral venue where people from different backgrounds can meet and where community relations courses and programmes take place. I coordinate and run the programmes with the aim of promoting reconciliation and improving community relations in this area.

Some of the successful programmes have looked at themes like sectarianism, religion and politics.

We are currently involved in several exciting projects including a joint Alpha course, a women's programme and organising a trip for young people to Baltimore in America to work on a charity project.

END OF UNIT REVIEW

End of Unit Questions

Look at the two adverts below which appeared in the Lisburn Inter-Church project's newsletter.

ALIVE

is a four-week programme aimed at exploring our religious, cultural and political identities through fun activities and a number of outdoor pursuits.

The programme has been developed for young adults, 16–25 years, attached to local churches. It is an exciting opportunity to meet other young adults from different traditions and share opinions in a unique environment and discuss your similarities and differences through a fun, interactive atmosphere.

If you are interested in joining this exciting project programme, please contact Lisburn Inter-Church today!

It's never too late to get ALIVE!!

Exploring Our Denominations

A major programme for the autumn looking at most of the Christian denominations in Lisburn and is led by local clergy.

The denominations we hope to cover will include: Baptist, Church of Ireland, Catholic, Methodist, Presbyterian and a number of other locally-based denominations. The series will conclude with a talk about the pros and cons of Inter-Church contact.

The series will run on Tuesday evenings, beginning in late September.

More info to follow.

In pairs, discuss the following:

1. How do you think the people attending each event might have benefited from the programme?

2. Do you think it is important to explore the similarities and differences between young people from different religious traditions?

3. In the 'Exploring our Denominations' advert, the series concluded with a talk on the pros and cons of inter-church contact. Imagine you were asked to give a similar talk and write a speech that you might give.

Learning outcomes

As a result of studying of this unit you should:

- understand some of the history of inter-church contacts in the ecumenical movement;

- explore different examples of inter-church contacts and reconciliation projects in N. Ireland;

- analyse different attitudes to inter-church contacts;

- reflect on the personal attitudes to religious similarities and differences.

Activity

Things shared, things different

What are the things that you share with others in your religious outlook? Use the following circle-time to explore some of the similarities and differences in your own class. You may have time to do all the activities at once or you may prefer to use different parts on different occasions.

It is also important that there is a significant amount of input from the group in developing the activities, so you may find you want to have several circle-times using your own ideas and suggestions for discussion.

Circle-time

- *Put the chairs in the room into a circle. It is important that the desks are pushed to the side.*

- *The purpose of the activity is primarily for everyone to contribute to a discussion, but before you begin, take time to establish some rules to ensure that everyone has a fair chance to speak, without having to shout, and in a way that they will be listened to with respect. These rules should be suggested by members of the group.*

- Identity game: *the purpose of the game is to realise the number of differences and similarities present even within a small group of people.*

  The game begins with one person standing in the middle of the circle, with everyone else seated. The person in the middle must say something about themselves which other people in the room might share in common. (For example, I like/dislike, I belong to, I agree/disagree with, etc.) All those people who identify with the statement as a similarity must change seats.

The person left standing must then make a statement about themselves. The game can continue for a set period of time or a set number of rounds.

- Group discussion: *the members of the circle must now discuss their feelings and thoughts about religious and cultural identity, using the rules already agreed by the group.*

  You might choose from some of the following statements as a stimulus or use some of your own.

  – *Ways in which I am similar to others*

  – *Ways in which I am different to others*

  – *How I think other people see me*

  – *How I would like other people to see me*

  – *The importance of religion to me*

  – *My view of others who do not share my religious beliefs*

  – *What I consider to be the difference between Protestants and Catholics*

  – *My feelings about religious education*

  – *My feelings about integrated education*

- Affirmation activity: *after your discussion, it is important to conclude on a positive note.*

  Each person in the group should have an opportunity to share a positive affirmation of someone else in the group or the group in general. (For example, "I appreciated the way people listened when I spoke" or "I didn't agree with Ann, but I admire her ability to state her point of view.")

- *You may also wish to make time for drawing conclusions from the whole circle-time. For example, has this activity taught you anything about accepting different viewpoints?*

INDEX